Scott Foresman
SCIENCE

Series Authors

Dr. Timothy Cooney
Professor of Earth Science and
  Science Education
Earth Science Department
University of Northern Iowa
Cedar Falls, Iowa

Michael Anthony DiSpezio
Science Education Specialist
Cape Cod Children's Museum
Falmouth, Massachusetts

Barbara K. Foots
Science Education Consultant
Houston, Texas

Dr. Angie L. Matamoros
Science Curriculum Specialist
Broward County Schools
Ft. Lauderdale, Florida

Kate Boehm Nyquist
Science Writer and Curriculum Specialist
Mount Pleasant, South Carolina

Dr. Karen L. Ostlund
Professor
Science Education Center
The University of Texas at Austin
Austin, Texas

Contributing Authors

Dr. Anna Uhl Chamot
Associate Professor and
  ESL Faculty Advisor
Department of Teacher Preparation
  and Special Education
Graduate School of Education
  and Human Development
The George Washington University
Washington, DC

Dr. Jim Cummins
Professor
Modern Language Centre and
  Curriculum Department
Ontario Institute for Studies in Education
Toronto, Canada

Gale Philips Kahn
Lecturer, Science and Math Education
Elementary Education Department
California State University, Fullerton
Fullerton, California

Vincent Sipkovich
Teacher
Irvine Unified School District
Irvine, California

Steve Weinberg
Science Consultant
Connecticut State
  Department of Education
Hartford, Connecticut

PEARSON
Scott
Foresman

Editorial Offices: Glenview, Illinois • Parsippany, New Jersey • New York, New York
Sales Offices: Boston, Massachusetts • Duluth, Georgia • Glenview, Illinois
Coppell, Texas • Sacramento, California • Mesa, Arizona

Content Consultants

Dr. J. Scott Cairns
National Institutes of Health
Bethesda, Maryland

Jackie Cleveland
Elementary Resource Specialist
Mesa Public School District
Mesa, Arizona

Robert L. Kolenda
Science Lead Teacher, K-12
Neshaminy School District
Langhorne, Pennsylvania

David P. Lopath
Teacher
The Consolidated School District
of New Britain
New Britain, Connecticut

Sammantha Lane Magsino
Science Coordinator
Institute of Geophysics
University of Texas at Austin
Austin, Texas

Kathleen Middleton
Director, Health Education
ToucanEd
Soquel, California

Irwin Slesnick
Professor of Biology
Western Washington University
Bellingham, Washington

Dr. James C. Walters
Professor of Geology
University of Northern Iowa
Cedar Falls, Iowa

Multicultural Consultants

Dr. Shirley Gholston Key
Assistant Professor
University of Houston-Downtown
Houston, Texas

Damon L. Mitchell
Quality Auditor
Louisiana-Pacific Corporation
Conroe, Texas

Classroom Reviewers

Kathleen Avery
Teacher
Kellogg Science/Technology Magnet
Wichita, Kansas

Margaret S. Brown
Teacher
Cedar Grove Primary
Williamston, South Carolina

Deborah Browne
Teacher
Whitesville Elementary School
Moncks Corner, South Carolina

Wendy Capron
Teacher
Corlears School
New York, New York

Jiwon Choi
Teacher
Corlears School
New York, New York

John Cirrincione
Teacher
West Seneca Central Schools
West Seneca, New York

Jacqueline Colander
Teacher
Norfolk Public Schools
Norfolk, Virginia

Dr. Terry Contant
Teacher
Conroe Independent
School District
The Woodlands, Texas

Susan Crowley-Walsh
Teacher
Meadowbrook Elementary School
Gladstone, Missouri

Charlene K. Dindo
Teacher
Fairhope K-1 Center/Pelican's Nest
Science Lab
Fairhope, Alabama

Laurie Duffee
Teacher
Barnard Elementary
Tulsa, Oklahoma

Beth Anne Ebler
Teacher
Newark Public Schools
Newark, New Jersey

Karen P. Farrell
Teacher
Rondout Elementary School
District #72
Lake Forest, Illinois

Anna M. Gaiter
Teacher
Los Angeles Unified School District
Los Angeles Systemic Initiative
Los Angeles, California

Federica M. Gallegos
Teacher
Highland Park Elementary
Salt Lake School District
Salt Lake City, Utah

Janet E. Gray
Teacher
Anderson Elementary - Conroe ISD
Conroe, Texas

Karen Guinn
Teacher
Ehrhardt Elementary School - KISD
Spring, Texas

Denis John Hagerty
Teacher
Al Ittihad Private Schools
Dubai, United Arab Emirates

Judith Halpern
Teacher
Bannockburn School
Deerfield, Illinois

Debra D. Harper
Teacher
Community School District 9
Bronx, New York

Gretchen Harr
Teacher
Denver Public Schools - Doull School
Denver, Colorado

Bonnie L. Hawthorne
Teacher
Jim Darcy School
School Dist #1
Helena, Montana

Marselle Heywood-Julian
Teacher
Community School District 6
New York, New York

Scott Klene
Teacher
Bannockburn School 106
Bannockburn, Illinois

Thomas Kranz
Teacher
Livonia Primary School
Livonia, New York

Tom Leahy
Teacher
Coos Bay School District
Coos Bay, Oregon

Mary Littig
Teacher
Kellogg Science/Technology Magnet
Wichita, Kansas

Patricia Marin
Teacher
Corlears School
New York, New York

Susan Maki
Teacher
Cotton Creek CUSD 118
Island Lake, Illinois

Efraín Meléndez
Teacher
East LA Mathematics Science
Center LAUSD
Los Angeles, California

Becky Mojalid
Teacher
Manarat Jeddah Girls' School
Jeddah, Saudi Arabia

Susan Nations
Teacher
Sulphur Springs Elementary
Tampa, Florida

Brooke Palmer
Teacher
Whitesville Elementary
Moncks Corner, South Carolina

Jayne Pedersen
Teacher
Laura B. Sprague
School District 103
Lincolnshire, Illinois

Shirley Pfingston
Teacher
Orland School Dist 135
Orland Park, Illinois

Teresa Gayle Rountree
Teacher
Box Elder School District
Brigham City, Utah

Helen C. Smith
Teacher
Schultz Elementary
Klein Independent School District
Tomball, Texas

Denette Smith-Gibson
Teacher
Mitchell Intermediate, CISD
The Woodlands, Texas

Mary Jean Syrek
Teacher
Dr. Charles R. Drew Science
Magnet
Buffalo, New York

Rosemary Troxel
Teacher
Libertyville School District 70
Libertyville, Illinois

Susan D. Vani
Teacher
Laura B. Sprague School
School District 103
Lincolnshire, Illinois

Debra Worman
Teacher
Bryant Elementary
Tulsa, Oklahoma

Dr. Gayla Wright
Teacher
Edmond Public School
Edmond, Oklahoma

ISBN: 0-328-26834-8

2008 Edition
Copyright © 2003, Pearson Education, Inc.
All Rights Reserved. Printed in the United States of America. This publication is protected by Copyright, and permission should be obtained from the publisher prior to any prohibited reproduction, storage in a retrieval system, or transmission in any form by any means, electronic, mechanical, photocopying, recording, or otherwise. For information regarding permission(s), write to: Permissions Department, Scott Foresman, 1900 East Lake Avenue, Glenview, Illinois 60025.

1 2 3 4 5 6 7 8 9 10 V057 13 12 11 10 09 08 07 06

 **Activity and Safety Consultants**

Laura Adams
Teacher
Holley-Navarre Intermediate
Navarre, Florida

Dr. Charlie Ashman
Teacher
Carl Sandburg Middle School
Mundelein District #75
Mundelein, Illinois

Christopher Atlee
Teacher
Horace Mann Elementary
Wichita Public Schools
Wichita, Kansas

David Bachman
Consultant
Chicago, Illinois

Sherry Baldwin
Teacher
Shady Brook
Bedford ISD
Euless, Texas

Pam Bazis
Teacher
Richardson ISD
   Classical Magnet School
Richardson, Texas

Angela Boese
Teacher
McCollom Elementary
Wichita Public Schools USD #259
Wichita, Kansas

Jan Buckelew
Teacher
Taylor Ranch Elementary
Venice, Florida

Shonie Castaneda
Teacher
Carman Elementary, PSJA
Pharr, Texas

Donna Coffey
Teacher
Melrose Elementary - Pinellas
St. Petersburg, Florida

Diamantina Contreras
Teacher
J.T. Brackenridge Elementary
San Antonio ISD
San Antonio, Texas

Susanna Curtis
Teacher
Lake Bluff Middle School
Lake Bluff, Illinois

Karen Farrell
Teacher
Rondout Elementary School,
   Dist. #72
Lake Forest, Illinois

Paul Gannon
Teacher
El Paso ISD
El Paso, Texas

Nancy Garman
Teacher
Jefferson Elementary School
Charleston, Illinois

Susan Graves
Teacher
Beech Elementary
Wichita Public Schools USD #259
Wichita, Kansas

Jo Anna Harrison
Teacher
Cornelius Elementary
Houston ISD
Houston, Texas

Monica Hartman
Teacher
Richard Elementary
Detroit Public Schools
Detroit, Michigan

Kelly Howard
Teacher
Sarasota, Florida

Kelly Kimborough
Teacher
Richardson ISD
   Classical Magnet School
Richardson, Texas

Mary Leveron
Teacher
Velasco Elementary
Brazosport ISD
Freeport, Texas

Becky McClendon
Teacher
A.P. Beutel Elementary
Brazosport ISD
Freeport, Texas

Suzanne Milstead
Teacher
Liestman Elementary
Alief ISD
Houston, Texas

Debbie Oliver
Teacher
School Board of Broward County
Ft. Lauderdale, Florida

Sharon Pearthree
Teacher
School Board of Broward County
Ft. Lauderdale, Florida

Jayne Pedersen
Teacher
Laura B. Sprague School
District 103
Lincolnshire, Illinois

Sharon Pedroja
Teacher
Riverside Cultural
   Arts/History Magnet
Wichita Public Schools USD #259
Wichita, Kansas

Marcia Percell
Teacher
Pharr, San Juan, Alamo ISD
Pharr, Texas

Shirley Pfingston
Teacher
Orland School Dist #135
Orland Park, Illinois

Sharon S. Placko
Teacher
District 26, Mt. Prospect
Mt. Prospect, IL

Glenda Rall
Teacher
Seltzer Elementary
USD #259
Wichita, Kansas

Nelda Requenez
Teacher
Canterbury Elementary
Edinburg, Texas

Dr. Beth Rice
Teacher
Loxahatchee Groves
   Elementary School
Loxahatchee, Florida

Martha Salom Romero
Teacher
El Paso ISD
El Paso, Texas

Paula Sanders
Teacher
Welleby Elementary School
Sunrise, Florida

Lynn Setchell
Teacher
Sigsbee Elementary School
Key West, Florida

Rhonda Shook
Teacher
Mueller Elementary
Wichita Public Schools USD #259
Wichita, Kansas

Anna Marie Smith
Teacher
Orland School Dist. #135
Orland Park, Illinois

Nancy Ann Varneke
Teacher
Seltzer Elementary
Wichita Public Schools USD #259
Wichita, Kansas

Aimee Walsh
Teacher
Rolling Meadows, Illinois

Ilene Wagner
Teacher
O.A. Thorp Scholastic Acacemy
Chicago Public Schools
Chicago, Illinois

Brian Warren
Teacher
Riley Community Consolidated
   School District 18
Marengo, Illinois

Tammie White
Teacher
Holley-Navarre
   Intermediate School
Navarre, Florida

Dr. Mychael Willon
Principal
Horace Mann Elementary
Wichita Public Schools
Wichita, Kansas

Inclusion Consultants

Dr. Eric J. Pyle, Ph.D.
Assistant Professor, Science Education
Department of Educational Theory
   and Practice
West Virginia University
Morgantown, West Virginia

Dr. Gretchen Butera, Ph.D.
Associate Professor, Special Education
Department of Education Theory
   and Practice
West Virginia University
Morgantown, West Virginia

Bilingual Consultant

Irma Gomez-Torres
Dalindo Elementary
Austin ISD
Austin, Texas

Bilingual Reviewers

Mary E. Morales
E.A. Jones Elementary
Fort Bend ISD
Missouri City, Texas

Gabriela T. Nolasco
Pebble Hills Elementary
Ysleta ISD
El Paso, Texas

Maribel B. Tanguma
Reed and Mock Elementary
San Juan, Texas

Yesenia Garza
Reed and Mock Elementary
San Juan, Texas

Teri Gallegos
St. Andrew's School
Austin, Texas

Unit A
Life Science

Go to HUMAN BODY UNIT D Table of Contents

Unit B
Physical Science

**Go to HUMAN BODY
UNIT D Table of Contents**

Unit C
Earth Science

Go to HUMAN BODY UNIT D Table of Contents

Unit D
Human Body

Here is the Table of Contents

Your Science Handbook

Using Scientific Methods for Science Inquiry

Scientists try to solve many problems. Scientists study problems in different ways, but they all use scientific methods to guide their work. Scientific methods are organized ways of finding answers and solving problems. Scientific methods include the steps shown on these pages. The order of the steps or the number of steps used may change. You can use these steps to organize your own scientific inquiries.

State the Problem

The problem is the question you want to answer. Curiosity and inquiry have resulted in many scientific discoveries. State your problem in the form of a question.

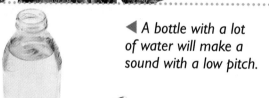

Does the amount of water in a bottle affect the pitch of the sound the bottle makes?

Formulate Your Hypothesis

Your hypothesis is a possible answer to your problem. Make sure your hypothesis can be tested. Your hypothesis should take the form of a statement.

◀ A bottle with a lot of water will make a sound with a low pitch.

Identify and Control the Variables

For a fair test, you must select which variable to change and which variables to control. Choose one variable to change when you test your hypothesis. Control the other variables so they do not change.

▲ Use four bottles of the same size. Leave the first bottle empty. Put a little water in the second bottle. Fill the third bottle halfway. Fill the fourth almost full with water.

Test Your Hypothesis

Do experiments to test your hypothesis. You may need to repeat experiments to make sure your results remain consistent. Sometimes you conduct a scientific survey to test a hypothesis.

Tap each bottle gently with a spoon. ▼

Collect Your Data

As you test your hypothesis, you will collect data about the problem you want to solve. You may need to record measurements. You might make drawings or diagrams. Or you may write lists or descriptions. Collect as much data as you can while testing your hypothesis.

Lower   High   Lowest   Low

Interpret Your Data

By organizing your data into charts, tables, diagrams, and graphs, you may see patterns in the data. Then you can decide what the information from your data means.

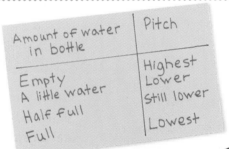

Amount of water in bottle	Pitch
Empty	Highest
A little water	Lower
Half full	Still lower
Full	Lowest

State Your Conclusion

Your conclusion is a decision you make based on evidence. Compare your results with your hypothesis. Based on whether or not your data supports your hypothesis, decide if your hypothesis is correct or incorrect. Then communicate your conclusion by stating or presenting your decision.

Bottles with more water make a sound with a lower pitch.

Inquire Further

Use what you learn to solve other problems or to answer other questions that you might have. You may decide to repeat your experiment, or to change it based on what you learned.

▲ *Does the size of the bottle make a difference in the pitch of a sound?*

Using Process Skills for Science Inquiry

These 12 process skills are used by scientists when they do their research. You also use many of these skills every day. For example, when you think of a statement that you can test, you are using process skills. When you gather data to make a chart or graph, you are using process skills. As you do the activities in your book, you will use these same process skills.

Observing

Use one or more of your senses—seeing, hearing, smelling, touching, or tasting—to gather information about objects or events.

I see..., I smell..., I hear..., It feels like..., I never taste without permission!

Communicating

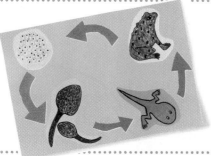

Share information about what you learn using words, pictures, charts, graphs, and diagrams.

Classifying

Arrange or group objects according to their common properties.

◄ Living things in Group 1.

Nonliving things in Group 2. ▶

Estimating and Measuring

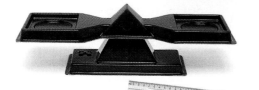

Make an estimate about an object's properties, then measure and describe the object in units.

Inferring

Draw a conclusion or make a reasonable guess based on what you observe, or from your past experiences.

The juice was cold this morning... It's still cold... The bottle is an...

Predicting

Form an idea about what will happen based on evidence.

◀ *Predict what will happen after 15 minutes.*

Making Operational Definitions

Define or describe an object or event based on your experiences with it.

A simple machine has no parts that move and it helps... ▶

Making and Using Models

Make real or mental representations to explain ideas, objects, or events.

◀ *It's different from a real food chain because... The model is like a real food chain because...*

Formulating Questions and Hypotheses

Think of a statement that you can test to solve a problem or to answer a question about how something works.

If you put one bean seed in loam and another one in sand, the plant will grow better in... ▶

The seed grew better in loam.

Collecting and Interpreting Data

Gather observations and measurements into graphs, tables, charts, or diagrams. Then use the information to solve problems or answer questions.

Identifying and Controlling Variables

Change one factor that may affect the outcome of an event while holding other factors constant.

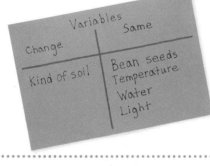

Experimenting

Design an investigation to test a hypothesis or to solve a problem. Then form a conclusion.

I'll write a clear procedure so that other students could repeat the experiment.

Science Inquiry

Throughout your science book, you will ask questions, do investigations, answer your questions, and tell others what you have learned. Use the descriptions below to help you during your scientific inquiry.

Does soup powder dissolve faster in hot water or cold water?

1 Ask a question about objects, organisms, and events in the environment.

You will find the answer to your question from your own observations and investigations and from reliable sources of scientific information.

2 Plan and conduct a simple investigation.

The kind of investigation you do depends on the question you ask. Kinds of investigations include describing objects, events, and organisms; classifying them; and doing a fair test or experiment.

3 Use simple equipment and tools to gather data and extend the senses.

Equipment and tools you might use include rulers and meter sticks, compasses, thermometers, watches, balances, spring scales, hand lenses, microscopes, cameras, calculators, and computers.

4 Use data to construct a reasonable explanation.

Use the information that you have gathered to answer your question and support your answer. Compare your answer to scientific knowledge, your experiences, and the observations of others.

5 Communicate investigations and explanations.

Share your work with others by writing, drawing, or talking. Describe your work in a way that others could repeat your investigation.

Question
Does soup powder dissolve faster in warm or cold water?

Materials
pack of soup powder
two plastic foam cups
warm water
cold water
two spoons

Unit D
Human Body

Science and Technology
In Your World!

Superman Isn't the Only One with X-Ray Vision!

Since X rays were discovered about 100 years ago, doctors have used them to look inside patients' bodies. But old-fashioned X-ray pictures have a flaw: They're flat, and most body parts aren't! Today, machines can beam X rays into the body at many different angles, making a series of flat pictures. A computer, like those used to make computer-animated movies, puts the flat pictures together to form a three-dimensional picture. As the picture slowly spins on the computer screen, doctors can study an entire body part, such as a bone. You will learn about bones and other body parts in **Chapter 1 The Body's Systems.**

Robots Test New Medicines!

Robots help scientists make and test thousands of substances in their search for new medicines. Following scientists' directions, some robots can make and test hundreds of substances in a single day. Powerful computers quickly analyze the results and help scientists decide what to try next. Rapid testing means that new medicines can reach your drugstore faster than ever before. You will learn about medicines in **Chapter 2 Staying Healthy.**

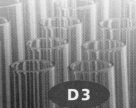

What's Inside?

X rays and other special pictures help doctors look inside you. But you don't have to be a doctor to learn how your body works. Just turn the page!

lung

heart

lung

liver

stomach

large intestine

small intestine

Chapter 1
The Body's Systems

Inquiring about The Body's Systems

Lesson 1
What Parts Make Up Your Body?

- What are the body's systems?
- What parts make up the body's systems?
- What are organs and tissues made of?

Lesson 2
How Do Bones and Muscles Work?

- What is the job of the skeletal system?
- How does a broken bone heal?
- How do joints help you move?
- What do muscles do?
- How do muscles help you move?
- What are the different kinds of muscles?

Lesson 3
What Are Some Other Body Systems?

- Why are your heart and blood vessels important?
- What jobs do your brain and nerves do?
- Why are your lungs and breathing important?
- What do your stomach and intestines do?

Copy the chapter graphic organizer onto your own paper. This organizer shows you what the whole chapter is all about. As you read the lessons and do the activities, look for answers to the questions and write them on your organizer.

Exploring Balance

Process Skills	**Materials**
• observing • inferring	• clock with a second hand

Explore

1 You will be testing your balance. Your partners will stand by to make sure you don't fall. As you do the test, **observe** how your muscles work to help you keep your balance.

2 Stand with your feet together and with your arms out. Have another student time how long you can stand with one foot off the floor. Put your foot down when needed to avoid falling. Record the time.

3 Repeat the test with your arms out and eyes closed.

Reflect

1. In which test did you keep your balance longer?

2. How did your muscles work to help you keep your balance?

3. Make an **inference.** What are some parts of your body that help you keep your balance?

? Inquire Further

Can you improve the time you can balance on one foot by practicing? Develop a plan to answer this or other questions you may have.

Using Graphic Sources

When you read a book, you might get some information from **graphic sources**, which are pictures, diagrams, or graphic organizers. These items can help you understand or organize the material. They also might show things that you would not be able to see. Most pictures in this book also have a **caption** that helps explain the picture. As you read the following chapter, *The Body's Systems,* think about the information you find in the graphic sources.

Reading Vocabulary

graphic sources (graf′ik sôrs′iz), pictures or diagrams that give information

caption (kap′shən), written material that helps explain a picture or diagram

Example

The picture is part of the photo on pages D8-D9. Part of its caption says, "Body systems work as a team to support life." The chart below lists some other graphic sources in Lesson 1, "What Parts Make Up Your Body?" Make a chart like this one on your own paper. As you read Lesson 1, look at the graphic sources. Write a sentence from each caption that connects the picture with the text.

Graphic Sources	Sentence from Caption
1. page D11: Body Systems	
2. page D12: Microscope	
3. page D13: Cells and tissues	

Talk About It!

1. How can graphic sources give information?

2. What graphic sources can you make to help you understand and organize information?

You will learn:

- about your body's systems.
- what parts make up the body's systems.
- what makes up organs and tissues.

Glossary

system (sis′təm), a group of body parts that work together to perform a job

What Parts Make Up Your Body?

A quick pass brings the ball to you. You kick. You score! Of course, you didn't win this soccer game by yourself. All the players on your team helped. The parts of your body work as a team too.

The Body's Systems

A **system** is a group of body parts that work together to perform a job. Several different systems make up the human body. Like each player on a team, each system of your body has its own special task to do.

On a soccer team such as the one shown here, some players score points. Other players defend the goal. In your body, one system allows you to breathe in and out. Another system turns the food you eat into fuel that your body can use. A different system carries blood through your body. Other systems hold you upright, help you move about, and allow you to read and understand the words in this book.

To win games, soccer players must work as a team. Your body systems work together too. Every minute of every day, the different systems of your body work as a team to keep you alive and healthy.

A group of players work as a team to win games. Body systems work as a team to support life. ▼

Glossary

organ (ôr′gən), a body part that does a special job within a body system

Choose one of the body systems shown in the students' drawings. Tell everything you already know about that system and about the organs that make it up. ▶

Parts That Make Up Body Systems

You probably know that you have a heart, a stomach, and two lungs. Each of those body parts is an **organ.** If you could see inside your body, you would have no trouble telling the organs apart. Your heart looks very different from your stomach, your lungs, and all of your other organs. Your heart also does its own special job of pumping blood. No other organ does that. Each organ in your body has its own special job.

Digestive system

Nervous system

Skeletal system

Each of your body systems is made of organs. Your heart is an organ of the circulatory system. Your stomach is an organ of the digestive system. Your lungs are organs of the respiratory system.

Other body systems include the skeletal system, muscular system, and nervous system. Organs in each system work together and depend on each other. You can see six body systems on these pages.

Circulatory system

Muscular system

Respiratory system

Glossary

Parts That Make Up Organs and Tissues

Each organ in your body is made of two or more kinds of tissue. A **tissue** is a group of cells that look alike and work together to do a certain job. **Cells** are the basic units, or building blocks, of the human body. In fact, all living things are made of cells.

Your body has millions and millions of cells. Cells are tiny. To see a cell, you must look through a microscope like the one on this page.

You have hundreds of different kinds of cells in your body. Muscle cells, nerve cells, and bone cells are three examples. Find the pictures of those cells on the next page. Notice that each has a different shape.

A microscope is a special tool that makes things look larger than they really are. Microscopes help scientists and students study tiny things such as cells. ▶

Muscle cells form muscle tissue. Your muscles change their shape to help you move about.

Nerve cells form nerve tissue. Your brain and nerves are made of nerve tissue. Your brain controls what you think and do. It gets and sends messages along nerves.

Bone cells form bone tissue. Your bones hold you up. Bones also work with muscles to help you move. Some bone cells also produce blood cells.

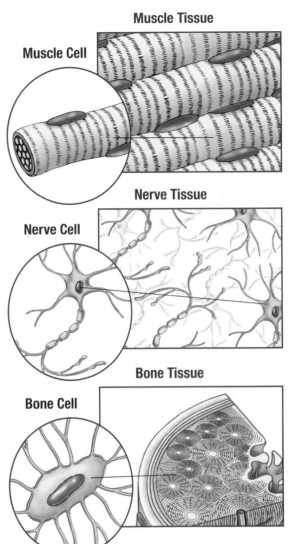

Muscle Tissue

Muscle Cell

Nerve Tissue

Nerve Cell

Bone Tissue

Bone Cell

▲ *Muscle cells and muscle tissue look different from nerve cells and nerve tissue, which look different from bone cells and bone tissue. Each kind of cell and tissue has a certain job to do.*

Lesson 1 Review

1. Tell two jobs that body systems do.
2. Name one organ in each of these body systems: circulatory system, digestive system, respiratory system.
3. What are organs made of, and what are tissues made of?
4. **Graphic Sources**
   Choose one of the groups of cells shown on this page. Make a diagram that shows how the cells are related to tissues, organs, and systems.

You will learn:

- about the job of the skeletal system.
- how a broken bone can heal.
- how your joints help you move.
- what muscles do.
- how your muscles help you move.
- about different kinds of muscles.

Lesson 2

How Do Bones and Muscles Work?

What can a hand puppet do when there is no hand inside it? Not much. It's so floppy that it collapses in a heap. Without bones and muscles, your body would be something like a floppy puppet.

The Skeletal System

About two hundred bones make up your body's skeleton, also called the skeletal system. Your skeleton does for your body what a hand does for a puppet like the one in the picture.

The bones of your skeleton help give shape to your body. Your bones also support you. Place a hand on one hip. The bone you feel is part of your pelvis. The bowl-shaped pelvis helps support your upper body when you sit and stand. Bones also work with muscles to help you move in all the ways that you do.

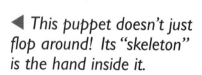

◄ *This puppet doesn't just flop around! Its "skeleton" is the hand inside it.*

Parts of the skeleton also protect your soft organs. Touch the top of your head. You can feel your skull, which protects your brain like a built-in helmet. Touch the ribs along your sides. The ribs form a cage that protects your heart and lungs.

Bones come in many shapes and sizes, as the picture of a skeleton shows. Bones are hard but not solid. They weigh less than you might expect. The longest and thickest bone in your body is the one between your hip and knee. Its strength helps hold you upright as you run and kick.

When you were born, your skeleton was made mostly of a rubbery tissue called **cartilage**. As you grow, bone replaces most of the cartilage. However, some cartilage remains. For example, your ears and the tip of your nose are made of cartilage. That is why you can bend them.

Glossary

cartilage (kär′tl ij), a tough, rubbery tissue that makes up parts of the skeleton

Glossary

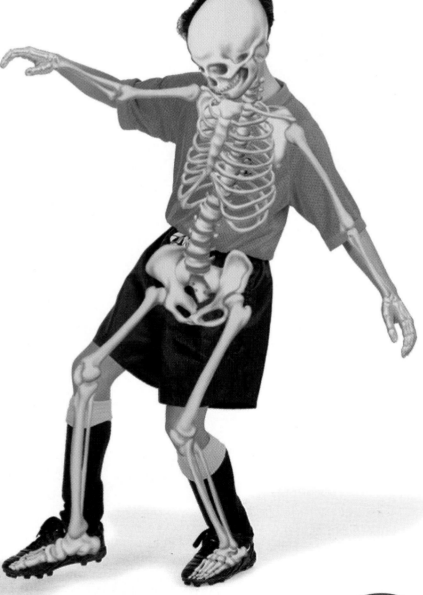

Life isn't all fun and games for your skeleton. It works hard to hold you up and help you move. ▼

How a Broken Bone Heals

Bones are strong. However, accidents can cause bones to break. Pictures called X rays help doctors see broken bones. Notice the X-ray picture of the broken bone.

Because it is living tissue, a broken bone can heal. A doctor can help the bone heal correctly by placing the injured part in a cast like the one shown. A cast holds a broken bone in the correct position while it mends.

Bone starts to mend soon after a break occurs. New bone cells begin to form. In a few days, spongy bone tissue fills the space between the broken ends of the bone. In the weeks that follow, the spongy tissue hardens until the bone is completely mended.

▲ The top X ray shows a bone broken below the knee. The bottom X ray shows the same bone after it mended.

A cast can be annoying, but it's necessary to help a broken bone heal correctly. ▶

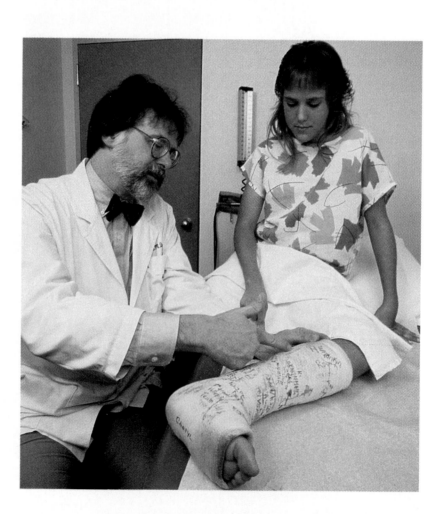

How Joints Help You Move

The place where two bones of the skeleton come together is called a **joint**. By themselves, bones are stiff. Joints allow movement. They give your skeleton its ability to bend, twist, and turn.

You have hinge joints in your elbows and knees. Find the pictures of those joints. Hinge joints work like door hinges. They let your arms and legs bend in one direction.

A layer of cartilage covers the ends of bones that meet at joints. The cartilage keeps the bones from grinding together and wearing out. Tissues called **ligaments** hold bones together at joints. You can see the ligaments of a knee joint below.

Glossary

Glossary

joint, the place where two bones come together

ligament (lig'ə mənt), a strong, flexible tissue that holds bones together at a joint

Elbow Joint

Hold one arm out. Swing the lower part away from you. Now swing it toward you. See how your elbow is like a door hinge? Open! Close! Open! Close!

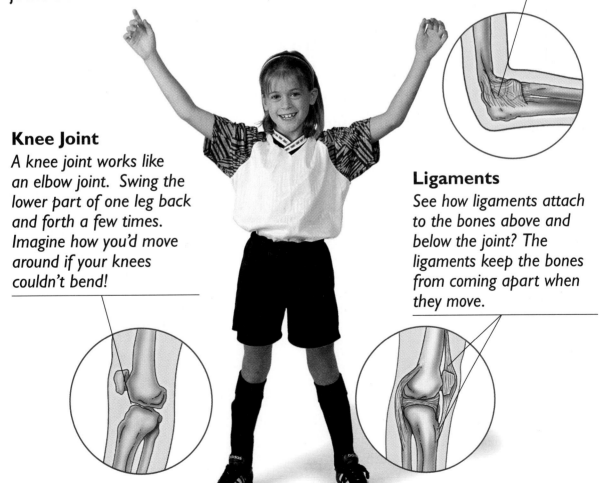

Knee Joint

A knee joint works like an elbow joint. Swing the lower part of one leg back and forth a few times. Imagine how you'd move around if your knees couldn't bend!

Ligaments

See how ligaments attach to the bones above and below the joint? The ligaments keep the bones from coming apart when they move.

Glossary

Glossary

muscle (mus′əl), body tissue that moves parts of the body

tendon (ten′dən), a strong cord of tissue that attaches a muscle to a bone

What Muscles Do

A **muscle** is a tissue made of muscle cells. Muscles have the job of making other body parts move. Muscles also help give your body its shape and help protect the soft organs inside you.

Your body's muscular system includes more than six hundred muscles. Most of those muscles move bones, allowing you to walk, lift, or kick a ball as the boy on the next page is doing.

Some muscles move body parts that are not bones. The muscles that move your eyebrows and lips help you smile, frown, or make a funny face. You can speak and sing because muscles move your lips, tongue, and lower jawbone.

Muscles are attached to bones by cords called **tendons**. You can feel a tendon at the back of each ankle. Find that tendon in the drawing on the next page.

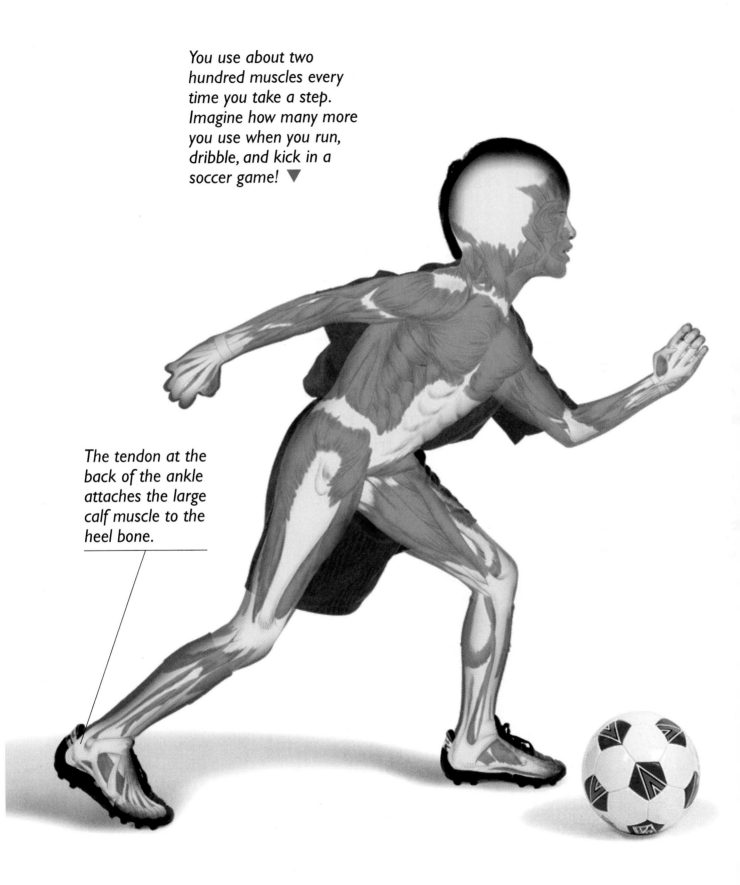

You use about two hundred muscles every time you take a step. Imagine how many more you use when you run, dribble, and kick in a soccer game! ▼

The tendon at the back of the ankle attaches the large calf muscle to the heel bone.

How Muscles Help You Move

Muscles can move bones because muscle cells can change their shape. Make a fist and lift it toward your shoulder. Notice how the muscle in your upper arm feels thick and hard. That is because the muscle cells contracted, or got shorter, to make the movement.

Muscles cannot push bones. Muscles can only pull. That is why muscles often work in pairs. One muscle pulls a bone one way. Another muscle pulls the bone the opposite way.

Look at the muscles in the picture. The top muscle in each upper arm is called the biceps. The muscle opposite the biceps is the triceps. When the biceps contracts, it pulls the boy's lower arm toward his shoulder. His arm bends. When the triceps contracts, it pulls the boy's lower arm away from his shoulder. His arm then straightens out.

Describe how the biceps and triceps of each arm look. ▼

Biceps

Triceps

Different Kinds of Muscles

Arm muscles are examples of **voluntary muscles.** You can control what they do and when they do it. Certain other muscles are **involuntary muscles.** They work without your control. They work even when you sleep. For example, the muscles that move food through your digestive system are involuntary muscles.

Your heart is a special kind of involuntary muscle. It looks something like a voluntary muscle and something like an involuntary muscle. However, it works without your control.

Some people have difficulty controlling their voluntary muscles. They may need special treatment or special tools, such as a wheelchair, to help them.

Glossary

voluntary
(vol′ən ter′ē)
muscle, the kind of muscle that a person can control

involuntary
(in vol′ən ter′ē)
muscle, the kind of muscle that works without a person's control

Glossary

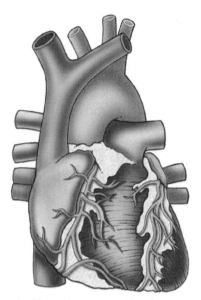

▲ *Your heart is the strongest muscle you have. It pumps blood through your body every single minute of every day.*

Lesson 2 Review

1. Tell two ways that the skeletal system helps the body.

2. Describe how a broken bone heals.

3. How do joints help you move?

4. What are two things that muscles do?

5. How do muscles help you move?

6. What are the differences between two kinds of muscles?

7. **Main Idea**
   Why is it important that your heartbeat and breathing are controlled by involuntary muscles?

Modeling How Muscles Work

Process Skills

- making and using models
- observing
- estimating and measuring

Materials

- safety goggles
- posterboard with shapes
- scissors
- hole punch
- sharpened pencil
- brass fastener
- 2 strings
- masking tape
- metric ruler

Getting Ready

Many muscles in your body work in pairs. In this activity you can demonstrate the way muscles work by making a model of muscles that move your foot.

Follow This Procedure

1 Make a chart like the one shown. Use your chart to record your observations and measurements.

2 Put on your safety goggles. Use scissors to cut out the shapes on the posterboard (Photo A). Use a hole punch to punch two holes at the top of shape A.

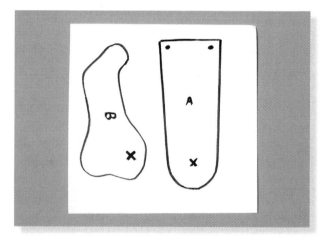

Photo A

3 Use a pencil to poke a hole through the X on each shape. Place shape B on top of shape A. Attach the two pieces with a brass fastener at letter X (Photo B).

	Direction that foot moves	Length of pulled string	Length of opposite string
String near toe pulled			
String near heel pulled			

Photo B

 Safety Note *Be careful when using pointed objects.*

4 Put a piece of string through each hole. Tape down one end of each piece of string as shown (Photo C). You have made a **model** of a foot and lower leg.

5 Pull the string that is closer to the toe of the foot. How does the foot move? **Measure** each string from the punched hole to where the string is taped. Record your **observations** and measurements.

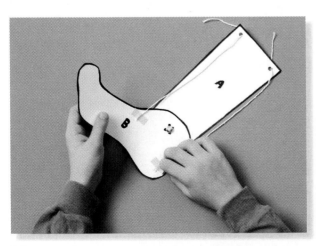

Photo C

6 Repeat step 5, but pull the string closest to the heel.

Interpret Your Results

1. What do the strings in the model represent?

2. What happened to the measured length of one string when you pulled on the opposite string? Describe how the strings act together to move the foot.

3. Compare and contrast your model to a real foot and leg.

Inquire Further

What actually happens to your leg muscles when you stand on your toes or stand back on your heels? Develop a plan to answer this or other questions you may have.

Self-Assessment

- I followed instructions to make a **model** of a foot and leg.
- I **observed** and **measured** how the strings in the model changed as the foot moved.
- I recorded my observations and measurements.
- I described the movement of the strings and how they affected the model.
- I compared and contrasted the model foot and leg to a real foot and leg.

You will learn:

- what your heart and blood vessels do.
- about your brain and nerves.
- about your lungs and breathing.
- what your stomach and intestines do.

Lesson 3

What Are Some Other Body Systems?

Most days, you pay little attention to how your body works. Today, though, you played a hard soccer game. Your lungs took in big gulps of air. Your heart raced. What else happened inside you, and why?

Heart and Blood Vessels

Your heart is a muscular organ that pumps blood. The blood travels to all parts of your body through tubes called blood vessels. Find the heart and blood vessels in the drawing. Your heart and blood vessels make up your circulatory system.

Blood brings oxygen and nutrients to cells. When you exercise, as the boy in the picture just did, your muscle cells need extra oxygen and nutrients. That is why your heart sometimes pumps fast.

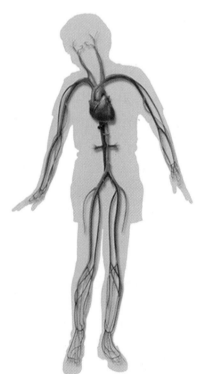

When you rest, your heart beats about ninety times a minute. It beats faster when you exercise. ▶

Brain and Nerves

You probably know that your brain controls your thoughts and feelings. Your brain also controls your actions, whether you're playing soccer or painting pictures as the boy below is doing. In fact, your brain controls heartbeat, breathing, and every other job your body does. Your brain works with your nerves. Together, the brain and nerves make up the nervous system.

You can see in the drawing that nerves thread their way throughout the body. Nerves carry messages between all parts of your body and your brain. If you need to take action, your brain sends a message along nerves to the correct muscles.

Your nervous system helps keep you safe. Suppose you touch a hot stove. Instantly, your nervous system signals your arm muscles to jerk your hand away. This fast action happens without your having to think about it.

▲ *Some nerves are thinner than a hair. Other nerves are thick. The long, very thick bundle of nerves that goes from the brain down the back is called the spinal cord.*

Your brain makes it possible for you to speak, read, write, remember, imagine, solve problems, and do hobbies such as drawing and painting. ▶

Lungs and Breathing

Your lungs and the tubes leading to them make up your respiratory system, shown below. Air enters your lungs each time you breathe in. Your body cells need oxygen from the air to stay alive. You breathe fast when you exercise because your muscle cells need extra oxygen. What other times do you breathe in an unusual way? (Hint: Look at the picture on the left.)

How does oxygen get from the air you breathe to your body cells? Oxygen in your lungs passes into your blood. Your heart pumps the blood to body cells. The blood delivers oxygen to the cells. The blood also picks up wastes that the cells have made, including a gas called carbon dioxide.

After the blood delivers its oxygen and picks up carbon dioxide, the blood is pumped back to your lungs. There, the blood gets rid of the carbon dioxide and picks up more oxygen. The carbon dioxide leaves your body when you breathe out.

▲ *Whoosh! The air you breathe out has more carbon dioxide and less oxygen than the air you breathe in.*

When you breathe in, air goes down a long tube called the windpipe. The windpipe divides into two tubes. One tube leads to each spongy lung. ▶

You may think you eat because you're hungry. Actually, you eat to stay alive, active, and healthy. Your digestive system changes food so that your cells can use it. ▶

Stomach and Intestines

A tasty meal like the one shown must be changed into a form that body cells can use for fuel. Your digestive system does this job. The system includes your stomach and intestines, shown below, which help break down food.

In your stomach, food is churned and mixed until it forms a liquid. In your small intestine, nutrients from the liquid pass into your blood. Your heart pumps the nutrient-rich blood to body cells. The parts of food that your body cannot use go into your large intestine. Later, these wastes leave your body.

Lesson 3 Review

1. What two important things does blood carry to body cells?

2. How is your brain connected with the rest of your body?

3. How does oxygen that is in the air get into your blood?

4. What happens to food in your stomach?

5. **Graphic Sources**
   Look at the caption for the top picture on page D25. What information does this caption give?

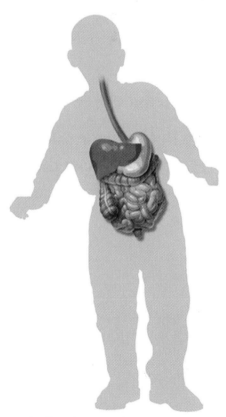

▲ *Food goes down a long tube to reach your stomach. Your intestines also are tubes, all curled up. The small intestine is longer, but narrower, than the large intestine.*

Observing Your Nervous System in Action

Process Skills

- observing
- inferring

Materials

- safety goggles
- half-meter stick

Getting Ready

In this activity you can find out more about your nervous system by testing your reaction time.

Follow This Procedure

1 Put on your safety goggles. Make a chart like the one shown. Use your chart to record your data.

	Distance half-meter stick fell
Trial 1	
Trial 2	
Trial 3	
Average distance	

2 Have a partner hold the half-meter stick vertically with the 0 end at the bottom. Hold your hands just below the stick as shown (Photo A).

3 Look closely at the half-meter stick as a partner gets ready to drop it.

Photo A

Photo B

④ When your partner drops the half-meter stick, catch it as quickly as you can. **Observe** how far the stick falls before you catch it by reading the number at the top of your hand (Photo B). Record the number in your chart.

⑤ Repeat steps 3 and 4 two more times.

⑥ Add the distances together and divide the total by 3 to get the average distance. Record your calculations.

Self-Monitoring
Did I record all my data and calculations?

Interpret Your Results

1. What was the average distance the half-meter stick fell before you caught it?

2. Look at the results for each trial. The lower the number, the faster is your reaction time. Which trial was your fastest?

3. Make an **inference.** What did your nervous system have to do from the moment your partner dropped the half-meter stick to the moment you caught it?

Inquire Further

Will your average reaction time become faster with practice? Develop a plan to answer this or other questions you may have.

Self-Assessment

- I followed instructions to **observe** how the nervous system works.
- I observed how far the half-meter stick fell before I caught it.
- I recorded my observations.
- I calculated the average distance the half-meter stick fell.
- I made an **inference** about how my nervous system works.

Chapter 1 Review

Chapter Main Ideas

Lesson 1

• Each body system has its own special job, but all body systems work together to support life.

• Each body system is made of organs, which work together and depend on each other.

• Organs are made of tissues, and tissues are made of cells, which are the building blocks of the body.

Lesson 2

• Bones help give shape to the body, support the body, help the body move, and protect organs.

• A broken bone heals by forming new bone cells and tissue.

• Bones come together at joints, allowing the skeleton to move.

• Muscles make body parts move, help give shape to the body, and help protect organs.

• Muscles move bones by changing shape and pulling on the bones.

• The body has both voluntary muscles and involuntary muscles.

Lesson 3

• The heart pumps blood through blood vessels to all parts of the body.

• The brain works with nerves to control thoughts and actions.

• The lungs take in air, which contains oxygen that the body needs, and also get rid of wastes.

• The stomach and small intestine change food into nutrients.

Reviewing Science Words and Concepts

Write the letter of the word or phrase that best completes each sentence.

a. cartilage g. organ

b. cell h. system

c. involuntary muscle i. tendon

  j. tissue

d. joint k. voluntary muscle

e. ligament

f. muscle

1. A body part that does a special job within a body system is an ___.

2. The kind of tissue formed by muscle cells is called ___.

3. A ___ is a flexible tissue that holds bones together at a joint.

4. The ___ is the basic unit of all living things.

5. A group of cells that look alike and work together is a ___.

6. The kind of muscle that a person can control is a ___.

7. A ___ is a group of organs that work together to perform a job.

8. An ___ is a kind of muscle that works without a person's control.

9. A ___ is a strong cord that attaches a muscle to a bone.

10. The ears and tip of the nose are made of a tissue called ___.

11. The place in the elbow where bones come together is a ___.

Explaining Science

Draw and label a picture or write a paragraph to answer these questions.

1. What makes up each of the following: a tissue, an organ, and a system?

2. How do the joint in your elbow and the muscles in your upper arm help you bend your arm?

3. Choose one body system: circulatory, nervous, respiratory, or digestive. What are the main parts of the system, and what job or jobs do they do?

Using Skills

1. **Use** the **graphic sources** below to answer the questions. Which picture shows a nerve cell and which shows nerve tissue? How can you tell?

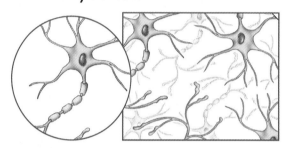

2. Sit with both knees bent and your feet flat on the floor. Straighten one leg so that it is sticking out in front of you. Then bend the leg so that it returns to where it was. What do you **infer** is happening with the muscles in your upper leg as you straighten and bend your leg?

Critical Thinking

1. Your six-year-old neighbor broke his leg a week ago. Now he's tired of wearing the cast and wants to take it off. He comes to you for help. **Apply** what you've learned about broken bones to this situation. Write what you will say to your young neighbor.

2. Make a **generalization.** When you are asleep, does your heart beat faster or more slowly than when you are awake? Explain your reasoning.

Good News!

It's exciting news when scientists invent a medicine. Here's some news that's even better: Most ways to stay healthy are a lot more fun than taking medicine!

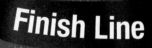

Finish Line

Chapter 2
Staying Healthy

Lesson 1
What Are Some Ways to Stay Healthy?

How do nutrients help your body?

How can you use the Food Guide Pyramid?

How does exercise help your body?

How can you exercise safely?

Why are rest and sleep important?

Inquiring about Staying Healthy

Lesson 2
What Are Germs?

What harm can some germs do?

How does the body fight disease germs?

How can you keep germs from spreading?

Lesson 3
How Do Some Substances Affect the Body?

How can people use medicines safely?

What are some harmful effects of alcohol?

What are some harmful effects of tobacco?

What are some harmful effects of illegal drugs?

Copy the chapter graphic organizer onto your own paper. This organizer shows you what the whole chapter is all about. As you read the lessons and do the activities, look for answers to the questions and write them on your organizer.

Exploring Food Choices

Process Skills
- classifying
- predicting

Materials
- pencil or marker
- paper

Explore

1 For two days, keep a "food diary" in which you list everything that you eat and drink each day. Include amounts, such as the number of bread slices you eat.

2 **Classify** the items from your food diary. Your teacher will give you the names of six groups. Make a chart by writing those names across the top of a large piece of paper. Write each item from your diary under the correct group name as shown.

Reflect

1. In which groups did you have the most items? the fewest items?

2. In this chapter you will learn about foods needed for good health. Make a **prediction.** Do you think your food choices will be considered healthy choices? Check your prediction as you learn about healthy food choices.

? **Inquire Further**

Do students your age make healthier food choices than older students do? Develop a plan to answer this or other questions you may have.

Making Pictographs

This tally table shows students' votes for their favorite breakfast foods. Make a **pictograph** to make the data easier to read.

Our Favorite Foods for Breakfast		
Food	**Tally**	**Number**
Fruit	II	2
Rice	IIII	4
Bagels	ℍℍ ℍℍ IIII	14
Cereal	ℍℍ ℍℍ ℍℍ ℍℍ ℍℍ ℍℍ ℍℍ ℍℍ II	42
Eggs	ℍℍ I	6
Pancakes	IIII	4

Materials
- grid paper

Math Vocabulary

pictograph
(pik′tə graf), a graph that uses pictures or symbols to show data

Remember

The key tells you what each symbol shows.

Work Together

1. Use grid paper to make a pictograph.

2. Decide what symbol to use on your pictograph. Have each symbol = 2 votes. Write a key for your pictograph.

3. Make sure your pictograph has a title.

4. How many symbols will you draw to show votes for cereal? How many symbols will you draw to show votes for bagels?

5. Complete your pictograph.

Talk About It!

How did you know how many symbols to draw for each breakfast food?

▼ *Mexican chiliquillas*

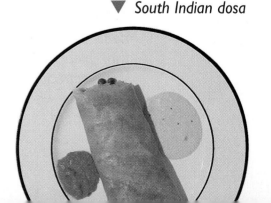

▼ *South Indian dosa*

You will learn:

- how nutrients help your body.
- how to use the **Food Guide Pyramid**.
- how exercise helps your body.
- how you can exercise safely.
- why rest and sleep are important.

Glossary

nutrient
(nü′trē ənt), a substance in food that living things need for health and growth

Lesson 1

What Are Some Ways to Stay Healthy?

Your body does amazing things! You can breathe, talk, and move around without even thinking about it. But to work its best, your body needs to be cared for. That takes some thought!

Nutrients and the Body

The people you see on these pages have thought about how to care for their bodies. They realize that eating healthful meals is important. Food contains **nutrients** that body cells need to live and do their work. Nutrients give the body energy. Nutrients help the body grow and repair itself. Nutrients also help the body work as it should.

◀ *This girl tries to eat healthful meals each day. She makes sure to drink plenty of water every day too. That's especially important in hot weather or when she is working or playing hard.*

Calcium is one nutrient you may have heard of. Calcium is important for growing strong bones and teeth. Milk, cheese, and yogurt are rich sources of calcium.

Did you know that water is a nutrient? Water brings other nutrients to cells and takes wastes away from cells. Water also helps keep your body temperature steady.

Some foods, such as milk, provide many different nutrients. However, no single food can give you all the nutrients your body needs. To stay healthy, you need to eat different kinds of food each day.

Like members of a team, the nutrients in different foods work together to help the body stay healthy. Do your part by eating a variety of foods. ▼

The Food Guide Pyramid

Look around any large grocery store, and you'll see hundreds of different foods. You may wonder how you can possibly choose the foods that will give you all the nutrients you need. An easy way to plan healthful meals is to use the Food Guide Pyramid shown on these two pages. It tells you how much of each kind of food to eat each day.

All of the parts of the Food Guide Pyramid—except fats, oils, and sweets—identify different food groups. Each group contains foods that have similar nutrients.

Look at the bottom of the pyramid. Notice the suggested servings for bread, cereal, rice, and pasta. What happens to the suggested serving size as you go up the pyramid?

Milk, Yogurt, and Cheese Group

Eat 2–3 servings each day. The foods in this group have many different kinds of nutrients. Your body uses these nutrients for growth and repair, energy, and working well.

Vegetable Group

Eat 3–5 servings each day. As with the Fruit Group, most of the nutrients in vegetables help your body work as it should.

Fats, Oils, and Sweets

Eat very little of these foods. These foods are not a food group. They can make a person gain too much body fat. In addition, sugary foods can cause tooth decay. Also, fatty foods are not good for the heart and blood vessels.

Meat, Poultry, Fish, Dry Beans, Eggs, and Nuts Group

Eat 2–3 servings each day. Most of the nutrients in these foods help your body grow and repair itself when needed.

Bread, Cereal, Rice, and Pasta Group

Eat 6–11 servings each day. Most of the nutrients in the foods in this group give your body energy.

Fruit Group

Eat 2–4 servings each day. As with the Vegetable Group, most of the nutrients in fruits help your body work as it should.

POPCORN

RICE

PASTA

YOGURT

Exercise and the Body

Making healthful food choices is one way to help your body. The children on these two pages know another way: exercise!

Exercise helps your muscles. When you exercise regularly, the cells in your voluntary muscles get bigger. As muscle cells get bigger, the whole muscle gets bigger and stronger.

Try to exercise every day. Activities such as in-line skating and tennis are good exercise, but you also can exercise by doing chores. Exercising with a friend or family member is fun, but you don't need a partner to be active. You don't need special equipment. You don't even need to leave your house!

Your heart is a special kind of muscle. It gets stronger when you exercise regularly. The muscles that help you breathe in and out get stronger too. As a result, your lungs work better.

Taking walks and playing active games are just two ways to get the exercise you need for good health. Regular exercise helps you feel better and look better. It helps you work and play without getting too tired. It even helps you sleep better at night! What kinds of exercise do you enjoy now? What new kind of exercise would you like to try?

How to Exercise Safely

Exercise is fun, but not if you hurt a muscle or have an accident. One way to prevent muscle injuries is to warm up before exercising. Do slow stretches to get your muscles ready for exercise. After you exercise, do the same kinds of stretches to help your muscles cool down. The chart has more ideas for keeping safe when you exercise.

Some Rules for Safe Exercise

- Choose a safe place to exercise. Be sure you have enough room to move around.

- Ask a responsible adult to show you the right way to do an exercise. Some exercises can be harmful if not done correctly.

- Wear comfortable clothes that let you move freely.

- Wear shoes that support your feet and fit correctly. Rubber-soled shoes are a good choice for most sports and games.

- Keep your shoes tied. You could trip over an untied shoelace.

- Wear proper safety equipment—such as a helmet, wrist protectors, kneepads, and elbow pads—for the activity you are doing. In-line skating, skateboarding, bicycling, and softball are some activities that require safety equipment.

- Drink water before and after exercise. If you exercise for a long time, take water breaks during your exercise. This is especially important in hot weather.

Rest and Sleep

No one can be active all the time. After you work or play hard, your body needs to recover. Reading a book, as the girl in the picture likes to do, is one way to rest your body.

Sleep is a special kind of rest. Like the boy below, you need to get plenty of sleep each night. Sleep helps you grow, because your body makes new cells more quickly when you are asleep. Other body activities slow down during sleep. Because your body uses less energy when you sleep, you'll have lots of energy for the next day.

Reading, playing a quiet game, and listening to music are some ways to give your body a rest. What do you do to rest? ▼

▲ *Going to bed on time is important. You can work, play, and learn better when you get enough sleep.*

Lesson 1 Review

1. Why does your body need the nutrients in food?

2. What food group should you eat the most servings from each day?

3. What does regular exercise do for your heart?

4. Why should you warm up before you exercise?

5. Why does sleep help you grow?

6. **Make Pictographs**
   Make a pictograph showing the foods you ate today from each group in the Food Guide Pyramid.

Testing Foods for Fat

Process Skills

- observing
- inferring

Materials

- piece of paper bag
- marker
- pat of butter
- paper towel
- carrot stick
- piece of raw potato
- potato chip
- other assorted foods

Getting Ready

In this activity you can test foods to see if they contain fat.

Fat is a nutrient in many foods. People need some fat in their diets, but eating too much fat can be harmful.

Follow This Procedure

1 Make a chart like the one shown. Use your chart to record your observations.

Food	Observation of spot	Presence of fat
Butter	Light shines through	Yes
Carrot	No light shines through	No
Raw potato		
Potato chip		

2 Use the marker to draw a circle on the paper bag for each food you will test. Each circle should be the size of a large coin.

⚠️ **Safety Note** *Do not taste any of the foods, either before or after testing them.*

3 Label one circle *Butter.* Rub the butter over the circle. Then wipe your hands with a paper towel. Hold the paper up to the light (Photo A). You will see light shining through the spot. This is caused by the fat in the butter.

Photo A

Photo B

④ Label another circle *Carrot.* Rub the carrot stick over the circle (Photo B). Wipe your hands with the paper towel. If the carrot makes a wet spot, let it dry. Hold the paper up to the light. There should be no light shining through the spot because carrots do not contain fat.

⑤ Repeat step 4 for each food. Wipe your hands on the paper towel after testing each food. **Observe** any spot made by the food. Record your observations.

⑥ Record whether or not fat was present in each of the foods. Wash your hands after this activity.

Interpret Your Results

1. Which of the foods were low in fat? Which were high in fat?

2. Potato chips are made by frying potatoes in oil. Make an **inference.** How does frying foods in oil change the amount of fat in the food?

**Inquire Further**

What meals could make up a low-fat menu for a week? Develop a plan to answer this or other questions you may have.

Self-Assessment

• I followed instructions to test foods for fat.
• I **observed** each food item's circle for its fat amount.
• I recorded my observations.
• I identified foods that are low in fat and high in fat.
• I made an **inference** about how frying foods in oil changes the amount of fat in the food.

You will learn:

- how some germs can be harmful.
- how the body fights disease germs.
- how to keep germs from spreading.

Glossary

germ (jėrm), a thing too tiny to be seen without a microscope; some may cause disease

disease (də zēz′), an illness

Here you see the germs that cause colds (left) and strep throat (right). The picture of the strep-throat germs has been enlarged 8,000 times. The picture of the cold germs has been enlarged 90,000 times. Influenza (flu), pneumonia, chicken pox, measles, and mumps are some other diseases caused by germs. ▶

Lesson 2

What Are Germs?

You can't see them, but they're everywhere! They're in air, water, soil, and food. They're on everything you touch. They're even on your skin and inside your body! What are they?

Germs and Disease

If you haven't guessed, they're germs. **Germs** are tiny things—so tiny that they must be viewed through a microscope. Many germs cause no harm. However, some germs cause disease. A **disease** is an illness. Many diseases caused by germs can spread from person to person. The pictures show two kinds of disease germs.

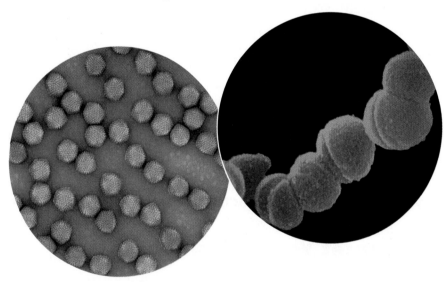

Fighting Disease Germs

To cause disease, germs must get in the body and make more germs. Your body has ways of keeping germs out. Your skin stops many germs from getting in. If you breathe germs in, hairs in your nose trap many of them. A sticky substance in your nose and throat also traps germs. You get rid of the germs when you sneeze, cough, or blow your nose.

Sometimes germs do get in. For example, a cut in the skin can let germs in. Then special blood cells go to work. Some cells surround and destroy germs. Other cells make substances that help destroy germs. Still other cells "remember" to make those substances if germs of the same kind get in the body again.

Medicines called **vaccines** can prevent certain diseases caused by germs. Some vaccines are given as shots. Other vaccines are swallowed. The child in the picture is getting a vaccine.

Glossary

vaccine (vak sēn′), a medicine that can prevent the disease caused by one kind of germ

Glossary

◄ Vaccines help the body fight disease germs. Each vaccine causes blood cells to "remember" to make the substances that attack one kind of germ. If that germ enters your body, the substances will attack it right away. You won't get sick. Your doctor knows what vaccines you should get.

How to Keep Germs from Spreading

Wash Those Hands!

Washing gets rid of germs. When your hands are clean, you're less likely to get germs on things that others might touch or put in their mouths. You're also less likely to get other people's germs into your own body. ▼

If you have disease germs in or on your body, you can spread them to other people. Germs may go into the air when you cough or sneeze. Germs may get onto things such as food, dishes, and pencils. The germs may enter the bodies of other people when they breathe or put things in their mouths. To help keep germs from spreading, do what the children in the pictures do.

Use Lots of Soap!

Don't just run your hands under the water for a few seconds. Wash your hands thoroughly after doing any activity that gets them dirty. Also, wash after you touch an animal, after you go to the bathroom, and before you handle or eat food. ▶

◀ **Use a Tissue!**
Cover your mouth and nose with a clean tissue whenever you cough or sneeze. Then throw the tissue away and wash your hands.

▲ **Don't Share Germy Stuff!**
Use your own drinking glass, toothbrush, towel, and washcloth. Never use someone else's fork, spoon, or dish without washing it first.

Lesson 2 Review

1. What are two diseases caused by germs?

2. Describe one way that the body fights germs.

3. Why is it important to wash your hands often?

4. **Identify the Main Idea**
   Read pages D 48 and D 49 again. Write a sentence that tells the main idea of these two pages.

D 49

You will learn:

- how people can use medicines safely.
- some harmful effects of alcohol.
- some harmful effects of tobacco.
- some harmful effects of illegal drugs.

How Do Some Substances Affect the Body?

Even if you've heard a lot about drugs, you may have questions like these: Is a medicine a drug? What's the harm in drinking or smoking? Why are some drugs against the law? You'll find the answers in this lesson.

Using Medicines Safely

The answer to the first question is yes, a medicine is a drug. A drug is a substance that causes changes in the body. Some medicines prevent disease. Other medicines help sick people, like the child in the picture, get well or feel better. However, any medicine can be harmful if used the wrong way. All medicines must be used with care.

◄ Only a responsible adult should give medicine to a child.

A **prescription medicine** is one that people need a doctor's order to buy. A pharmacist fills the order and puts a label on the medicine, like the one in the picture. Only the person whose name is on the label should take the medicine. The adult who takes or gives the medicine should follow the directions on the label exactly.

An **over-the-counter medicine** is one that people can buy without a doctor's order. It is just as important to follow the label directions on an over-the-counter medicine as on a prescription medicine. The chart has some more ideas for using medicines safely.

Glossary

prescription medicine
(pri skrip′shən med′ə sən), a medicine that can be bought only with a doctor's order

over-the-counter medicine, a medicine that can be bought without a doctor's order

Some Rules for Safe Medicine Use

- Do not take any medicine by yourself. Take medicine only from a doctor, a nurse, or an adult responsible for you.

- Leave the labels on all medicines. That way, people know what the medicine is and what directions to follow.

- Never share prescription medicines. One person's medicine might make another person sick.

- Tell an adult responsible for you if you feel any unwanted effects from a medicine, such as an upset stomach or a headache.

- Keep medicines away from small children, and keep medicine containers closed.

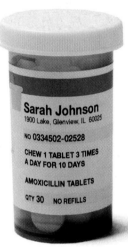

▲ *Directions on a prescription medicine label may include how much medicine to take, when to take it, and how long to take it.*

Glossary

alcohol (al′kə hȯl), a drug found in beer, wine, and liquor that can be harmful

Alcohol upsets the way the brain and body work. This baseball player could not perform well or be safe if she had alcohol in her body. ▼

Harmful Effects of Alcohol

Beer, wine, and liquor are drinks that contain alcohol. **Alcohol** is a drug. It can be harmful to a person's health and safety.

Alcohol goes to the brain very quickly. Alcohol changes the way a person's brain works. A person who drinks alcohol may have trouble thinking and talking clearly. The person also may walk unsteadily, feel dizzy or sleepy, and have trouble seeing clearly. A person who often drinks large amounts of alcohol can damage his or her body organs. However, the person may find it hard to stop drinking.

Alcohol makes it impossible to do many activities safely. Playing baseball is just one example of such an activity. Riding a bicycle or driving a car after drinking alcohol can lead to a serious accident.

Harmful Effects of Tobacco

Cigarettes, cigars, chewing tobacco, and pipe tobacco are made from the tobacco plant. Tobacco contains a drug called **nicotine**. Nicotine can harm the heart. Tobacco users are more likely to get heart disease than other people. Nicotine also makes it hard for a tobacco user to quit.

Tobacco smoke contains dark, sticky tar and other substances that can harm the lungs. Smokers are more likely to get lung cancer and other lung diseases than other people. Tobacco smoke also may harm the health of people who are around smokers and breathe in the smoke.

Glossary

nicotine (nik′ə tēn′), a drug in tobacco that can harm the body

Glossary

◀ A person needs a strong heart and lungs to keep going for a long time. Smoking can harm the heart and lungs. Smokers may find it hard to do activities such as running or swimming. After a short time, they may be out of breath and too tired to continue.

Glossary

Glossary

illegal (i lē′ gəl)
drug, a drug that is
against the law to buy,
sell, or use

Harmful Effects of Illegal Drugs

Drugs that are against the law are called **illegal drugs.** These dangerous drugs include marijuana, heroin, and cocaine. Such drugs change the way the brain works. They can make a person feel very sick. They also can seriously damage body organs. Despite such effects, people who use illegal drugs usually find it hard to stop. Until a person reaches a certain age, alcohol and tobacco are also considered illegal drugs.

The students who attend the school in the picture want to stay healthy and safe. That is why they say "no" to all illegal drugs.

◀ *What does this sign tell you about this school?*

Lesson 3 Review

1. List three ways to use medicines safely.

2. What are two things that an alcohol drinker may have trouble doing?

3. What effects does nicotine have?

4. Why should people say "no" to drugs such as marijuana, heroin, and cocaine?

5. **Compare and Contrast**
   Compare and contrast prescription medicine and over-the-counter medicine.

Conducting a Sleep Survey

Materials

- four small pieces of paper
- numbered paper bag
- writing paper
- grid paper

Process Skills

- formulating questions and hypotheses
- identifying and controlling variables
- experimenting (survey)
- collecting and interpreting data
- communicating

State the Problem

How many hours of sleep do most third graders get?

Formulate Your Hypothesis

If you survey third graders about how much sleep they get each night, what answer will most of them give? Write your hypothesis.

Identify and Control the Variables

Control variables to conduct a fair survey. Each student must be asked the same question. Keep your answers private to avoid influencing other students' answers. Include all classmates in the survey.

Test Your Hypothesis

Follow these steps to conduct a survey.

1 Make a survey form like the one on the next page. Use the survey form to record your data.

2 Each student in your group should think about the following question: "How many hours of sleep do you get on a typical school night?"

3 Have each student in your group write an answer on a small piece of paper, fold the paper, and put it into the bag.

Continued ➜

④ Pass the bag to another group of students. Remove the slips of paper from the bag passed to your group. **Collect** and **record** your **data.** On your chart, make a tally mark by the number of hours of sleep written on each piece of paper. Put the slips of paper back in the bag.

⑤ Repeat step 4 until you have recorded data from all groups, including your own.

Collect Your Data

Number of hours of nightly sleep	Number of students
Less than 8	
8	
9	
10	
11	
12	
More than 12	

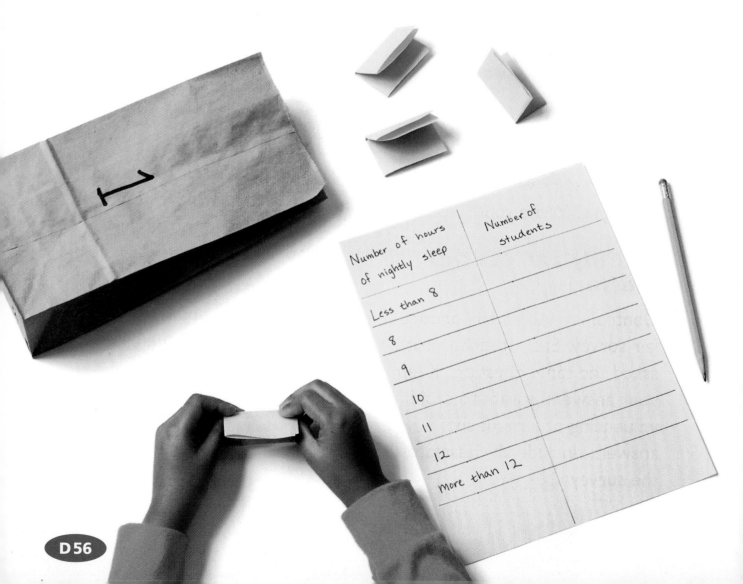

Interpret Your Data

1. Label a piece of grid paper as shown. Use the data from your chart to make a bar graph on your grid paper.

2. Study your graph. Tell how many hours of sleep the largest number of students reported.

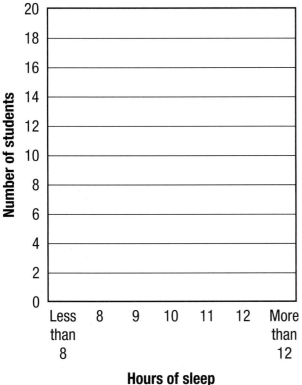

Hours of sleep

State Your Conclusion

How do your results compare with your hypothesis? **Communicate** your conclusion about how much sleep most third graders get. Discuss the results with your class.

 **Inquire Further**

How much sleep do younger students get? Make a plan to answer this or other questions you may have.

Self-Assessment

- I made a **hypothesis** about how much sleep most third graders get.
- I **identified** and **controlled variables.**
- I conducted an **experiment** (class survey) to test my hypothesis.
- I **collected data** in a chart and **interpreted** my **data** by making and studying a graph.
- I **communicated** by stating my conclusion.

Chapter 2 Review

Chapter Main Ideas

Lesson 1

• Nutrients in food give your body energy, help your body grow and repair itself, and help your body work as it should.

• The Food Guide Pyramid tells how much of each kind of food to eat each day to get all the nutrients needed.

• Exercise strengthens the voluntary muscles, the heart muscle, and the muscles that help with breathing.

• Ways to exercise safely include warming up before exercising and cooling down after exercising.

• Sleep is a special kind of rest that helps the body grow and saves energy for the next day's activities.

Lesson 2

• Some germs cause diseases, such as colds, strep throat, flu, pneumonia, chicken pox, measles, and mumps.

• Your body has several ways to keep germs out and to destroy germs that do get inside.

• Ways to keep germs from spreading include washing hands with soap and water, covering sneezes and coughs with tissues, and not sharing such items as drinking glasses.

Lesson 3

• Ways to use medicines safely include not sharing prescription medicines and following the directions on the label of any medicine.

• Alcohol changes the way the brain works, can lead to accidents, and can damage body organs over time.

• Tobacco can harm a smoker's heart and lungs and may harm the health of other people who breathe in the smoke.

• Illegal drugs such as marijuana, heroin, and cocaine change the way the brain works, can make people very sick, and can seriously damage body organs.

Reviewing Science Words and Concepts

Write the letter of the word or phrase that best completes each sentence.

a. alcohol

b. disease

c. germ

d. illegal drug

e. nicotine

f. nutrient

g. over-the-counter medicine

h. prescription medicine

i. vaccine

1. Any medicine that requires a doctor's order is a ___.

2. A ___ is a substance in food that is needed for health and growth.

3. A medicine that can prevent the disease caused by one kind of germ is a ___.

4. Tobacco contains ___.

5. A ___ is a tiny thing that may cause disease.

6. Medicine bought without a doctor's order is ___.

7. Beer, wine, and liquor contain a drug called ___.

8. Another word for illness is ___.

9. An ___ is any drug that is against the law.

Explaining Science

Make a chart or write a paragraph to answer these questions.

1. What can you do today to stay healthy? Include food, exercise, and sleep in your answer.

2. What will your body do to fight germs today?

3. What are some reasons to stay away from alcohol, tobacco, and illegal drugs? Give at least one reason for each.

Using Skills

1. Make a **pictograph** using the data below. Decide on a symbol to use, and have each symbol equal 3 votes. Be sure to include a title and a key.

Our Favorite Kinds of Exercise		
Exercise	Tally	Number
In-line skating	✝✝✝ /	6
Bicycling	✝✝✝ ✝✝✝ ✝✝✝	15
Basketball	✝✝✝ ////	9
Soccer	✝✝✝ ✝✝✝ ✝✝✝ ✝✝✝ /	21
Jumping rope	///	3
Dancing	✝✝✝ /	6

2. Even if your favorite food is a healthful one, such as milk or apples, would it be a good idea to eat only that food? Why or why not? **Communicate** your thoughts by writing a paragraph.

Critical Thinking

1. Gayle wants Robin to try a cigarette. Robin is not sure how to refuse while still keeping Gayle as a friend. **Solve the problem.** Write a note to Robin, suggesting what she might say to Gayle.

2. The directions on an over-the-counter medicine can no longer be read. What do you **conclude** is the best thing to do with the medicine? Explain your reasoning.

Unit D Review

Reviewing Words and Concepts

Choose at least three words from the Chapter 1 list below. Use the words to write a paragraph that shows how the words are related. Do the same for Chapter 2.

Chapter 1
cartilage
joint
ligament
muscle
tendon
voluntary muscle

Chapter 2
disease
germ
illegal drug
over-the-counter
 medicine
prescription
 medicine
vaccine

Reviewing Main Ideas

Each of the statements below is false. Change the underlined word to make each statement true.

1. A tissue is a group of <u>organs</u> that look alike and work together to do a certain job.

2. About two hundred <u>systems</u> make up the body's skeleton.

3. Muscles move bones by <u>pushing</u> them.

4. Your <u>stomach</u> works with your nerves to control your thoughts and actions.

5. The lungs and the tubes leading to them make up the <u>circulatory</u> system.

6. The body uses substances called <u>wastes</u> for energy, for growth and repair, and for working well.

7. Sleep is a special kind of <u>exercise</u>.

8. If you breathe germs in, hairs in your <u>mouth</u> trap many of them.

9. A <u>food</u> is any substance that causes changes in the body.

10. Cigarettes contain <u>alcohol</u>, which can harm the heart and make it hard to quit smoking.

Interpreting Data

Use the medicine label to answer the questions below.

1. Is this a prescription medicine or an over-the-counter medicine? How can you tell?

2. How often should this medicine be taken?

3. You are at a friend's house. Your ear starts to hurt. Your friend brings you this medicine and suggests that you take some. Why should you say no?

Communicating Science

1. Explain how body cells depend on the respiratory, digestive, circulatory, and nervous systems to stay alive. Write a paragraph.

2. Make a list of the ways that your bones help you.

3. How can a person get the nutrients that he or she needs each day? Use what you know about the Food Guide Pyramid to write an answer to that question.

4. Draw and label a picture that shows how the body keeps many germs out and fights germs that do get in.

Applying Science

1. What would your life be like if you had to think about making your involuntary muscles work? Write a diary entry for one day.

2. It's almost time for supper. Your hands look perfectly clean. Write a short paragraph that explains why you should wash your clean-looking hands before eating supper.

3. A child breaks her lower leg. When the cast finally comes off, the muscles of the lower leg are small and weak. Write a few sentences that explain why that happened and what the child can do about it.

4. Make a poster that a community group could use to discourage people from drinking alcohol.

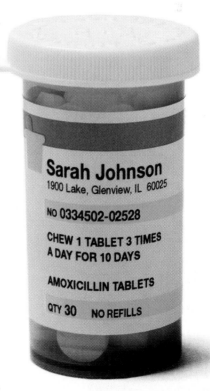

Sarah Johnson
1900 Lake, Glenview, IL 60025

NO 0334502-02528

CHEW 1 TABLET 3 TIMES
A DAY FOR 10 DAYS

AMOXICILLIN TABLETS

QTY 30   NO REFILLS

Unit D
Performance Review

Museum of the Body

Using what you learned in this unit, complete one or more of the following activities to be included in a Museum of the Body. The exhibits will help visitors learn more about body systems and staying healthy. You may work by yourself or in a group.

Body Art

Make an outline of the human body on a large sheet of paper. You might trace around a partner standing in front of paper fixed to a wall. Inside the outline, draw the circulatory system. Label the parts. If you wish, repeat for other body systems. Display your artwork in the museum.

Joint Demonstration

You've learned about hinge joints—now use your library to find out about the other joints your body has. Plan a demonstration about joints for the museum. Prepare a chart about joints to display. As you talk about each kind of joint, show the joint's movement with your own body.

A Sweet Poem

Think about your favorite kinds of fruit. Why do you like to eat them? How do they help your body? Turn your ideas into a poem titled "Fabulous Fruit." Plan to recite your poem for museum visitors. Put lots of feeling into it!

Health Pictographs

Make one or more pictographs for the museum's math room. The pictographs should show data that you have collected about your classmates' health practices. For example, you may have pictographs about how much sleep your classmates get and what kinds of exercise they do to stay healthy.

Puppet Play

The museum will have an exhibit just for children five years old and younger. Prepare a puppet play about stopping the spread of germs for this exhibit. Your puppets can be human or animal characters. You may also want to have a character named Mr. or Ms. Germ!

Using Graphic Organizers

A graphic organizer is a visual device that shows how ideas and concepts are related. Word webs, flowcharts, and tables are different kinds of graphic organizers. The graphic organizer below is an example of a flowchart. It shows how the parts of the human body you studied in Chapter 1 are related.

Make a Graphic Organizer

In Chapter 2, you learned about ways to keep the human body healthy. You also learned about substances that can harm the body. Use information in Chapter 2 to make a graphic organizer that shows what substances are harmful to the human body. Include information about how each substance is harmful.

Write a Persuasive Letter

Develop materials to convince younger children to stay away from substances that can be harmful to their bodies. Use information in your graphic organizer to write a persuasive letter or brochure for use with the children.

Remember to:

1. **Prewrite** Organize your thoughts before you write.

2. **Draft** Write your persuasive letter or brochure.

3. **Revise** Share your work and then make changes.

4. **Edit** Proofread for mistakes and fix them.

5. **Publish** Share your letter or brochure with your class.

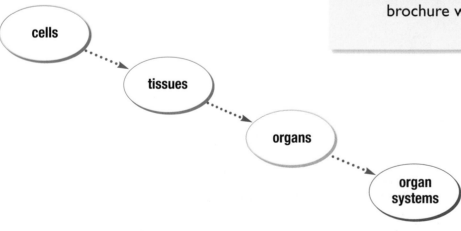

cells → tissues → organs → organ systems

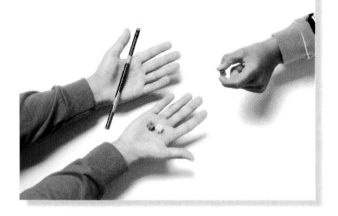

Your Science Handbook

 Safety in Science

Scientists know they must work safely when doing experiments. You need to be careful when doing experiments too. The next page shows some safety tips to remember.

Safety Tips

- Read each experiment carefully.
- Wear safety goggles when needed.
- Clean up spills right away.
- Never taste or smell substances unless directed to do so by your teacher.
- Handle sharp items carefully.
- Tape sharp edges of materials.
- Handle thermometers carefully.
- Use chemicals carefully.
- Dispose of chemicals properly.
- Put materials away when you finish an experiment.
- Wash your hands after each experiment.

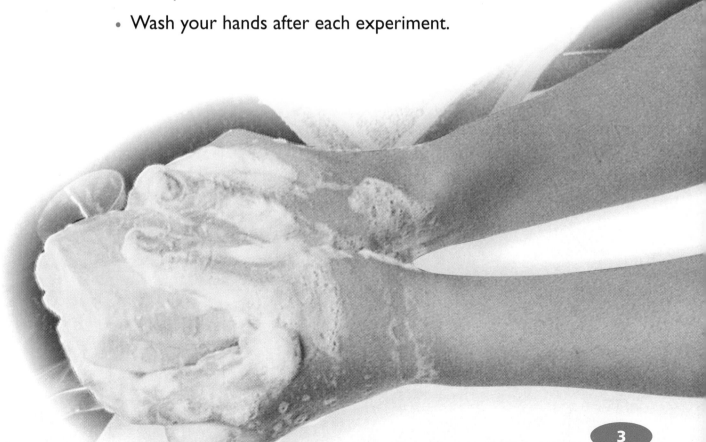

Using the Metric System

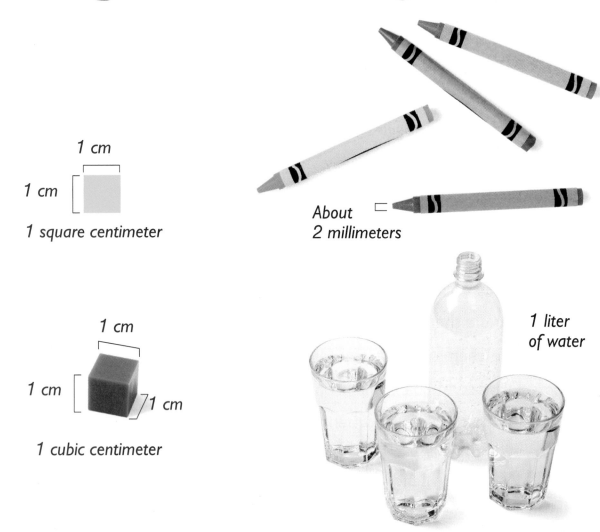

1 cm
1 cm

1 square centimeter

About
2 millimeters

1 cm
1 cm
1 cm

1 cubic centimeter

1 liter
of water

11 football fields end to end
is about 1 kilometer

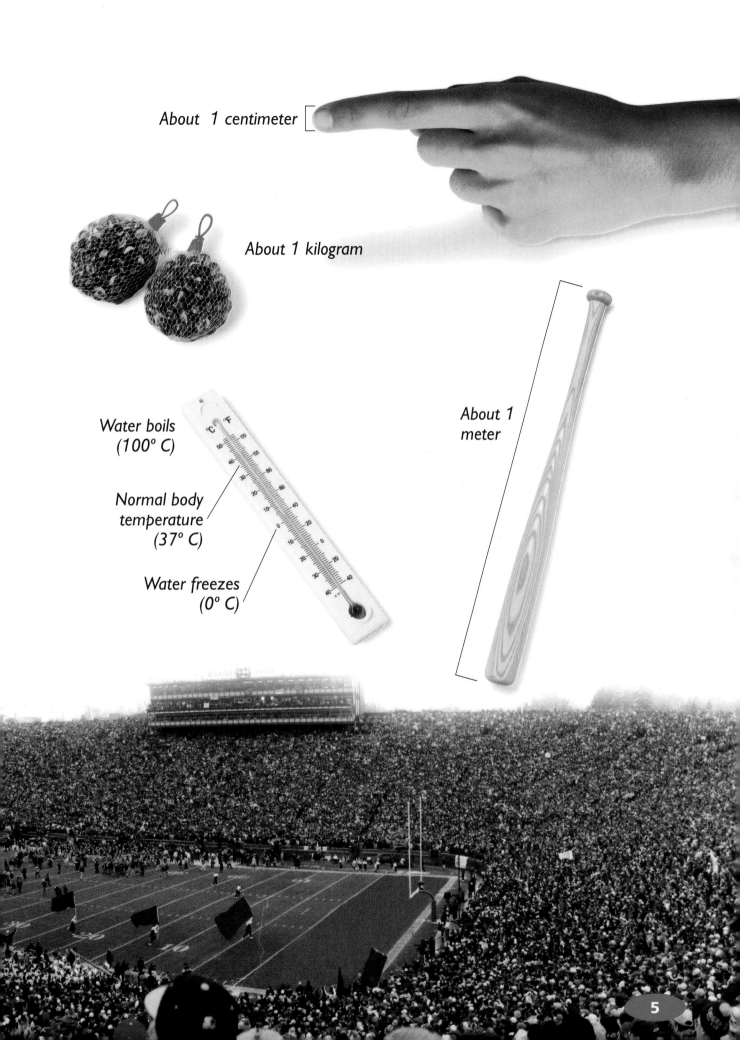

About 1 centimeter

About 1 kilogram

Water boils
(100° C)

Normal body
temperature
(37° C)

Water freezes
(0° C)

About 1
meter

Observing

How can you improve your observations?

There are different ways to observe things. The method you choose can affect how fully and accurately you notice and record things. Observation is a very important part of scientific investigation.

Observation involves the use of all five senses. Effective observing requires you to use your senses of sight, hearing, smell, and touch to gather information about objects and events. Taste is very important too, but you should never taste an unknown object—it could be dangerous!

When you are first observing something, you should be quiet and still. Then you can touch things, smell them, move them, shake them gently, and compare them with others.

Organizing your senses intelligently can help you make better observations.

Practice Observing

Materials

• small hand bell

Follow This Procedure

1. Sit quietly while you observe the bell with your eyes, ears, and nose. Do not taste or touch the bell.

2. List each sense and describe what you observed with it.

3. Touch the bell with your fingers. Move it on its side to observe all of its parts.

4. Pick the bell up and shake it.

5. Compare what you observed about the bell before you shook it with what you observed afterwards. What changed? What sense did you use to observe it?

6. Compare your bell with the bell of your partner. Do you observe any difference with your eyes, ears, or nose? Can you tell the two bells apart by observing them just with your sense of hearing?

7. Compare the size of your bell with your partner's bell. Observe the length, width, and height of the bells.

Thinking About Your Thinking

List the steps you used to learn about the shape, feel, and look of the bell.

List all of the steps you used to observe what happens when the bell makes a sound. How many senses did you use?

List the things you did to compare the size of your bell and your partner's bell.

Communicating

How do you communicate clearly?

You communicate when you use words, pictures, and body language to share what you observe.

To communicate the difference between two very similar things, you need to use clear, precise communication. Some forms of communication work better than others in different situations.

Putting accurate information into a table can help you to communicate more clearly.

Practice Communicating

Materials

- two transparent plastic containers
- distilled water
- olive oil
- magnifying glass
- paper towels

Follow This Procedure

1. Work in pairs.

2. First, on your own, observe the properties of the water and describe them in your journal. Describe its color or lack of color. Is it transparent? (Can you see through it?) How well? Describe its smell. Is it wet? Is it slippery? Is it slimy? Are things floating in it? Draw a picture of the water.

3. Make a table with a column to communicate your observations about water.

4. Repeat step 2 with olive oil. Use the paper towels to wipe up spills immediately. Wash your hands after touching the oil.

5. In your table, next to your water observations, add another column to communicate your observations about the olive oil.

6. Pick one liquid in your table. Read its properties to your partner until he or she can tell which liquid you are describing.

7. Reverse roles. Now your partner can pick one liquid in his or her table. Try to determine if your partner is describing water or oil.

8. Show each other your tables and compare them.

Thinking About Your Thinking

Why were drawings not very useful for telling water and oil apart?

Did creating a table make communication easier?

Think about the importance of clear communication. Imagine if you asked someone for a glass of chocolate and you got a glass of chocolate oil instead of chocolate milk! Sometimes communication must be exact!

Classifying

How can you recognize common properties?

Classifying means arranging or grouping objects according to their common properties.

To be a good classifier, you need to learn about, understand, and recognize the properties of objects. You also need to be able to create new ways to group objects.

Objects that you classify may have some properties in common but not others. As a result, they may be classified together in some groupings and not in others.

Developing an organized way to classify objects can be very helpful. With organization and practice, your classifying skills will be right on the money.

▲ 50 pennies

▲ 25 shiny pennies

Practice Classifying

Materials

- 5 pennies
- 2 nickels
- 2 foreign coins
- 10 dimes
- 4 quarters

Follow This Procedure

1 Work in groups of four.

2 Name one group, or classification, to which all of the objects belong. When you begin to classify a group of objects, you might look at the big groups that they belong to. The objects in front of you could be grouped as money, coins, or metals.

3 Which coins aren't used in the United States? Classify your coins in two groups: (1) U.S. coins and (2) foreign coins.

4 What is the name of the coin that is worth one cent? What coin is worth five cents? Ten cents? Twenty-five cents? Group the coins by name and record how many you have in each classification.

5 Create a classification called "worth a dollar." How many quarters would you need to put together to be in the "worth a dollar" group? How many dimes would you need?

Thinking About Your Thinking

What classification groupings did you use to separate the coins? Which coins do you use every day?

Coin collectors, or numismatists, classify coins in many other ways. A rare penny that is in excellent, or mint, condition, is worth much more than one cent to a collector. Some are worth thousands of dollars! In what other ways might you classify coins?

Estimating and Measuring

How can you estimate and measure correctly?

An estimate is your best guess about how heavy, how long, how tall, or how hot an object is.

Once you've estimated the object's properties, you can then measure and describe them in either metric or customary units.

For example, you can estimate the mass of a pencil. Put a pencil in one hand and a gram cube in the other hand. Estimate how many gram cubes will equal the mass of the pencil. Measure to see if your estimate was correct.

Practice Estimating and Measuring

Materials

- balance
- gram cubes
- classroom objects

Follow This Procedure

1 Make a chart like the one below.

Object	Estimated mass in grams	Actual mass in grams

2 Hold an object in one hand and gram cubes in the other.

3 Estimate the mass of the object in grams. Add and remove gram cubes from your hand to equal your estimate.

4 Place the object on one side of the balance and place gram cubes on the other side to find out the actual mass of the object in grams.

5 Record your data in the chart.

6 Repeat steps 2 to 5 for each object.

Thinking About Your Thinking

Which object has the most mass? Which object has the least mass? How close were your estimates to the actual masses?

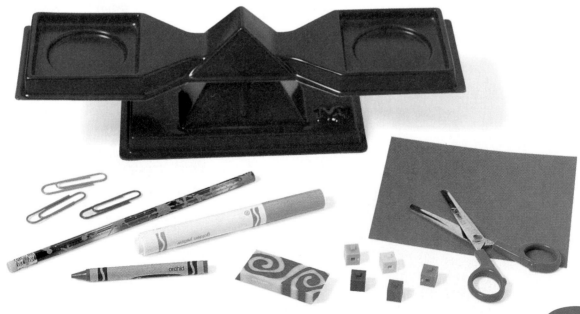

Inferring

How do you infer?

Has anyone ever asked you to make a guess about something? When you make a reasonable guess based on what you have observed or what you know, you are making an inference.

Look at the picture in this page. What is the girl pouring on the plant? How can you tell? What made you guess the way you did?

Practice Inferring

Materials

- *magnet* (labeled)
- metal bolt
- metal nails
- cardboard
- small wooden plank
- paper clips
- paper

Follow This Procedure

1 Take the object labeled *magnet* and test it with the metal objects. Observe if the object labeled *magnet* attracts the metal objects.

2 Infer from your observations and past experience if the object labeled *magnet* is a magnet.

3 Place a piece of paper over the metal objects. Observe if the *magnet* attracts the metal objects. Consider your observations and past experience. What can you infer about the *magnet* and the paper? Does the *magnet* attract objects through the paper?

4 Place a piece of cardboard over the metal objects. Observe if the *magnet* attracts the metal objects. Consider your observations and past experience. What can you infer about the *magnet* and the cardboard? Does the *magnet* attract objects through cardboard?

5 Place a piece of wood over the metal objects. Observe if the *magnet* attracts the metal objects. Consider your observations and past experience. What can you infer about the *magnet* and the wood? Does the *magnet* attract objects through wood?

Thinking About Your Thinking

List the steps you used to make an inference about how magnets attract through paper. Do you think it is always correct?

Can you infer from these observations that magnetic attraction never goes through wood? Just this magnet? Just this wood?

Predicting

How can you make predictions?

When you predict, you make a forecast about what will happen in the future. Predictions are based on what you have studied or observed.

Read each group of sentences below. On your own paper, predict what will happen.

A stalk of celery was put into a glass jar. The jar had red water in it. Think about what you know about plants. Predict what will happen.

It has rained all morning. A puddle is on the sidewalk. The sun comes out and the day is bright and warm. Predict what will happen to the puddle.

Practice Predicting

Materials

- 20 mL of water
- 100 mL graduated cylinder
- 25 marbles

Follow This Procedure

1 Make a chart like the one below.

Number of marbles	Prediction	Water Level in mL
0		
5		
10		
15		
20		
25		

2 Make a graph like the one below.

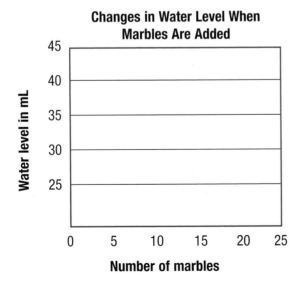

Changes in Water Level When Marbles Are Added

3 Pour 20 mL of water into the graduated cylinder.

4 Record the water level in the chart.

5 Tilt the cylinder and carefully drop 5 marbles into it. Record the water level in the chart.

6 Add 5 more marbles so you have 10 marbles in the cylinder. Again, record the water level.

7 Predict what the water level will be with 15 marbles. Predict what the water level will be with 20 marbles and with 25 marbles.

8 Test each of your predictions and record your results.

9 Fill in your graph with the data from your chart.

Thinking About Your Thinking

What do you think will be the water level of the cylinder if you added 30 marbles? 40 marbles? What did you use to make these predictions?

Making Operational Definitions

What is an operational definition?

An operational definition is a definition or description of an object or an event based on your experience with it.

For example, an operational definition of a clock is: an object that has hands and keeps time in hours.

As your experience changes, your operational definition may also change. For example, you then might give this definition of a clock: a device that keeps time electronically and has digital numbers.

A good operational definition can shed light on even the most difficult topics. Can you define the word "shadow" based on what you know about it?

Practice Making Operational Definitions

Materials

- flashlight
- meter stick or tape measure

Follow This Procedure

1. Write what you know about shadows. Are they light or dark? What causes their shapes? When don't you have a shadow?

2. Early in the morning, go out to the schoolyard as a class and look for your shadow. Have a classmate measure the length of your shadow.

3. Return to the same spot at noon and measure your shadow again. Is it shorter or longer? Is the sun higher or lower at noon than in the morning?

4. Explore making shadows with the flashlight and your fingers. Can you make the shadows longer or shorter? How?

5. Write an operational definition of the word "shadow" based on your experience.

Thinking About Your Thinking

Where is your shadow when there is no light? Did your operational definition help you to answer the question?

Making and Using Models

How can you make and use models?

A model is a small copy of something. Models are important tools for explaining ideas, objects, and events.

Anything that is not real but is a copy of an actual idea, object, or event can be called a model. There are four steps to making a model.

1. Learn all about an object or event.

2. Think about what you could do to make a copy of the object or event.

3. Make the model.

4. Compare your model to the actual object or event.

Practice Making and Using Models

Materials

- cardboard
- tape
- small rubber or plastic wheels
- paint brushes
- string
- paper
- scissors
- toothpicks
- plastic wrap
- paint
- fabric
- rubber bands

Follow This Procedure

1. Begin by imagining the model car you wish to build. Keep in mind the materials that are available. Draw your model car.

2. Start making the body of your model car. Do you want your car to be very light, or more sturdy? Do you want to be able to see everything inside of it?

3. Will your car have doors? If so, how many? Will there be a roof? Can the roof come off as in a convertible?

4. How will your car be powered? Where is the power source located?

5. Try moving the car without wheels. Will wheels make movement easier or more difficult? Add wheels to your model.

6. What color is your car? Paint your car or cover it with fabric.

Thinking About Your Thinking

How did making a model of a car help you to learn about real cars? What other models have you built?

Formulating Questions and Hypotheses

How can you formulate questions and hypotheses?

Scientific inquiry often begins with asking a question. Sometimes one question leads to an even more useful one. To answer your question, you formulate a hypothesis and design an experiment to test it.

Keep the question clearly in focus as you formulate your hypothesis. Testing a well thought out hypothesis will help you with your scientific inquiry.

Practice Formulating Questions and Hypotheses

Materials

- container of water
- 4 sponges
- construction paper
- graduated cylinder

Follow This Procedure

1. **Question:** How does the size of a sponge affect the amount of water it will hold? Write down your hypothesis or educated guess.

2. Make a chart like the one below.

Sponge size	Water left in cylinder (mL)	Water in sponge (mL)
2 cm x 2 cm		
3 cm x 3 cm		
4 cm x 4 cm		
5 cm x 5 cm		

3. Place the 2 cm × 2 cm sponge on a dry piece of construction paper.

4. Fill the graduated cylinder with water to the 250 mL mark.

5. Pour the water 10 mL at a time evenly over the sponge. Each time, lift the sponge. When the paper is wet, stop pouring. Record the amount of water left in the cylinder.

6. Subtract the amount of water left in the cylinder from 250 to find out how much water is in the sponge. Record this number in the chart.

7. Refill the graduated cylinder to 250 mL.

8. Repeat steps 3 - 7 with the remaining three sponges.

Thinking About Your Thinking

Did your investigation support your hypothesis? Explain.

Collecting and Interpreting Data

How do you collect and interpret data?

You collect data when you observe things and make measurements. The data can be put into graphs, tables, charts, or diagrams. You interpret data when you use the information to solve problems or to answer questions.

Rice cereal

Nutrition Facts		
Serving Size:		11/4 Cup (33g/1.2 oz.)
Servings per Package		About 16
Amount per Serving	Cereal	Cereal with 1/2 Cup Vitamins A & D Skim Milk
Calories	120	160
Fat Calories	0	0
% Daily Value**		
Total Fat 0g*	0%	0%
Saturated Fat 0g	0%	0%
Cholesterol 0mg	0%	0%
Sodium 350mg	15%	17%
Potassium 40mg	1%	7%
Total **Carbohydrates** 29g	10%	11%
Dietary Fiber 0g	0%	0%
Sugars 3g		
Other Carbohydrate 25g		
Protein 2g		

Wheat cereal

Nutrition Facts		
Serving Size:		1 Cup (29g/1.0 oz.)
Servings per Package		About 12
Amount per Serving	Cereal	Cereal with 1/2 Cup Vitamins A & D Skim Milk
Calories	110	150
Fat Calories	0	0
% Daily Value**		
Total Fat 0g*	0%	0%
Saturated Fat 0g	0%	0%
Cholesterol 0mg	0%	0%
Sodium 210mg	9%	11%
Potassium 35mg	1%	7%
Total **Carbohydrates** 25g	8%	10%
Dietary Fiber 1g	4%	4%
Sugars 3g		
Other Carbohydrate 21g		
Protein 2g		

Corn cereal

Nutrition Facts		
Serving Size:		1 Cup (31g/1.1 oz.)
Servings per Package		About 14
Amount per Serving	Cereal	Cereal with 1/2 Cup Vitamins A & D Skim Milk
Calories	120	160
Fat Calories	0	0
% Daily Value**		
Total Fat 0g*	0%	0%
Saturated Fat 0g	0%	0%
Cholesterol 0mg	0%	0%
Sodium 120mg	5%	8%
Potassium 25mg	1%	7%
Total **Carbohydrates** 28g	9%	11%
Dietary Fiber 0g	0%	0%
Sugars 14g		
Other Carbohydrate 14g		
Protein 1g		

Practice Collecting and Interpreting Data

Materials

- graph paper
- pencil

Follow This Procedure

1 Make a chart like the one shown. Look over the Nutrition Facts on each cereal box shown on the page on the left. Record the following data from each of them: amount per serving of sodium (in mg), protein (in g), and sugars (in g).

Amount per serving

Cereal	Sodium (mg)	Protein (g)	Sugars (g)
Wheat			
Rice			
Corn			

2 Based on the information in your chart, which cereals have the same amount of protein? Which cereal has the most sugars?

3 Make a bar graph that compares the amount of sodium in the three cereals. Use the graph below as a model.

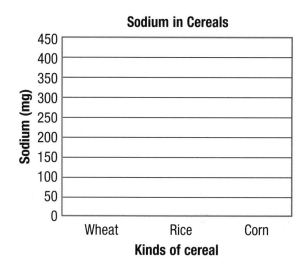

4 From your data, determine which cereal has the most sodium. Which has the least?

Thinking About Your Thinking

How might you use a bar graph to show the amount of potassium in each cereal?

Identifying and Controlling Variables

How do you identify and control variables?

A variable is anything that can change in an experiment. You identify and control variables when you change one variable that may affect the result of an experiment. You control the other variables by keeping them the same.

First you should decide which variable you wish to change. Then you identify all variables that you need to keep the same.

Practice Identifying and Controlling Variables

Materials

- 6 books
- ruler with groove down the middle
- marble
- metric tape measure

Follow This Procedure

1. Make a chart like the one below.

Height of ramp	Distance marble travels (cm)
1 book	
2 books	
3 books	
4 books	
5 books	
6 books	

2. Make a ramp by setting one end of the ruler on top of one of the books. Place the other end of the ruler on a lower, flat surface.

3. Roll the marble from the top of the ramp. Use the metric tape measure to measure the distance the marble travels from the end of the ramp.

4. Record the distance in your chart.

5. Add another book and roll the marble again. Measure the distance it travels from the end of the ramp.

6. Repeat this procedure until the ramp is 6 books high.

Thinking About Your Thinking

Which variable did you change? Which variable responded to the change, or, in other words, what did you measure? Which variables were kept the same?

Experimenting

How do you perform a scientific experiment?

In a scientific experiment, you design an investigation to try to solve a problem by testing a hypothesis. Based on the results, you draw conclusions.

Here are the steps in the process:

1. State the problem you are investigating.

2. Formulate a hypothesis about the problem.

3. Identify and control the variables. Decide which variables you will keep the same and which you will change.

4. Test your hypothesis in an experiment.

5. Collect your data.

6. Interpret your data.

7. State your conclusion. Did the data support your hypothesis?

Practice Experimenting

Materials

- safety goggles
- marble
- paper
- oil
- water
- two 50 mL cylinders
- stopwatch

Follow This Procedure

1. Think about solid objects falling through liquids, like a toy falling through bath water. Would the toy fall as quickly through oil? Which is thicker, oil or water?

2. State the problem. What factors affect the rate at which an object falls through a liquid?

3. Write a hypothesis about the thickness of a liquid and the time it would take for a marble to drop to the bottom of a cylinder filled with that liquid.

4. Design your experiment. The variable that will change is the type of liquid in the cylinder. The marble and the amount of liquid will be the variables that remain the same.

NOTE: *Gently* push the marble from the edge of each cylinder into the liquid. *Don't* throw it with any force.

5. Make a chart to record your data.

6. Put on your safety goggles. Perform your experiment. Record the time it takes for the marble to reach the bottom of the cylinder of each liquid. Do several trials for each liquid.

7. Interpret you data by making a graph based on information in your chart.

8. Make a conclusion about your hypothesis. Does the data support your hypothesis or prove it wrong?

Thinking About Your Thinking

List the seven steps in the logical process of performing a scientific experiment. Is their order important?

Kingdoms of Living Things

Scientists divide the millions of organisms that live on the earth into five groups called kingdoms. Organisms in each kingdom are like each other in some ways and are different from organisms in other kingdoms. The five kingdoms of living things are monerans, protists, fungi, plants, and animals.

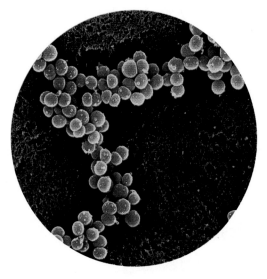

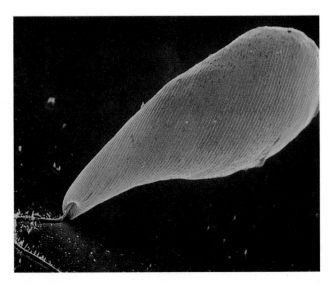

Monerans

▲ *Monerans are made of one cell. They are so small that they cannot be seen without a microscope. Bacteria and other one-celled organisms belong to this kingdom.*

Protists

▲ *Some protists are made of one cell. Others are made of many cells. Many protists have parts that help them move. Certain protists can make their own food while others must take in food. Most seaweeds are protists. Seaweeds are made of many cells and can make their own food.*

Animals

▲ *Like plants, animals are made of many cells. Animals cannot make their own food. Most animals can move from place to place.*

Fungi

▲ *Some fungi are one-celled organisms. Most fungi, however, are made of more than one cell. Fungi cannot make their own food. They absorb food made by other organisms. Molds, yeasts, and mushrooms are examples of fungi.*

Plants

Plants are made of many cells. Green plants use sunlight to make their own food. Plants cannot move from place to place. Their roots hold them tightly in the soil. ▼

Vertebrates and Invertebrates

The animal kingdom can be divided into two main groups. One group contains animals that have a backbone. Animals that have backbones are called vertebrates. The other group contains animals that do not have a backbone. These animals are called invertebrates.

▲ *Crabs belong to a group called crustaceans.*

Invertebrates

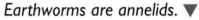

Earthworms are annelids. ▼

Spiders belong to a group of invertebrates called arachnids. ▶

The group to which sponges belong is known as porifera. ▼

▲ *Insects are the largest group of animals.*

◀ *Jellyfish are coelenterates.*

Vertebrates

◀ *Snakes, turtles, and lizards belong to a group called reptiles.*

▲ *A hummingbird is one of many different birds.*

Koalas are mammals. ▶

Frogs are amphibians. ▶

Sharks are fishes. ▶

Life Cycle of a Tree

The stages in the life cycle of a tree include seeds, germination, seedling, and growth and pollination. After a time, the tree dies, falls to the ground, and begins to rot, or decompose.

▲ A seed germinates when the tiny plant inside it begins to grow.

▲ A seed falls to the ground.

A seedling is a young plant. ▶

A fully grown plant makes flowers and seeds. ▼

▼ A dead tree falls to the ground and starts to decompose. Organisms such as ants, worms, and fungi are known as decomposers. They feed on the tree.

Mixtures and Solutions

Mixtures

A mixture is formed when two or more objects are mixed together, but each object keeps its own properties. You can easily separate the different parts that make up a mixture.

▲ A salad is a mixture. Even though all the parts taste good together, each piece has its own flavor.

◀ Pasta with sauce is a mixture. The sauce itself is a mixture too.

Solutions

A solution is a special kind of mixture. In a solution, two or more substances are evenly mixed together. We sometimes say that one material is dissolved in another. Some properties of some of the substances might change.

In soda water, a gas is dissolved in water. You cannot see the gas until it starts to separate from the water. When this happens, you see the gas as bubbles in the water. ▼

Ocean water is a solution that contains many minerals dissolved in water. ▼

Properties of Matter

Some properties of matter can be measured. Other properties cannot be measured but can be described. Color, size, and taste are some properties of matter. Magnetism, hardness, and density are also properties of matter.

▲ This rock, called a lodestone, is a mineral that is found in the earth. Lodestones are natural magnets. They will push together or pull apart from each other. Materials made of iron or with iron in them will be attracted or repelled by lodestones.

▲ You can tell how hard a material is by rubbing it against another material. The harder material will scratch the softer material. The objects shown here have different levels of hardness. The chalk is the softest, followed by the pencil lead, and then the penny. A diamond is the hardest mineral. It will scratch any other material. ▼

Density describes how much mass is in a certain amount of matter. The rubber duck and the metal car are about the same size. The density of the car is greater than the density of water. The density of the rubber duck is less than the density of water. Therefore, the rubber duck will float on the surface of the water while the car sinks to the bottom. ▼

Structure of Matter

All matter is made of smaller and smaller pieces, or particles. You cannot see the smallest particles of matter. An atom is the smallest whole bit of each kind of matter. Two or more atoms can join together to form larger particles. In the different states of matter, the particles are arranged in different ways.

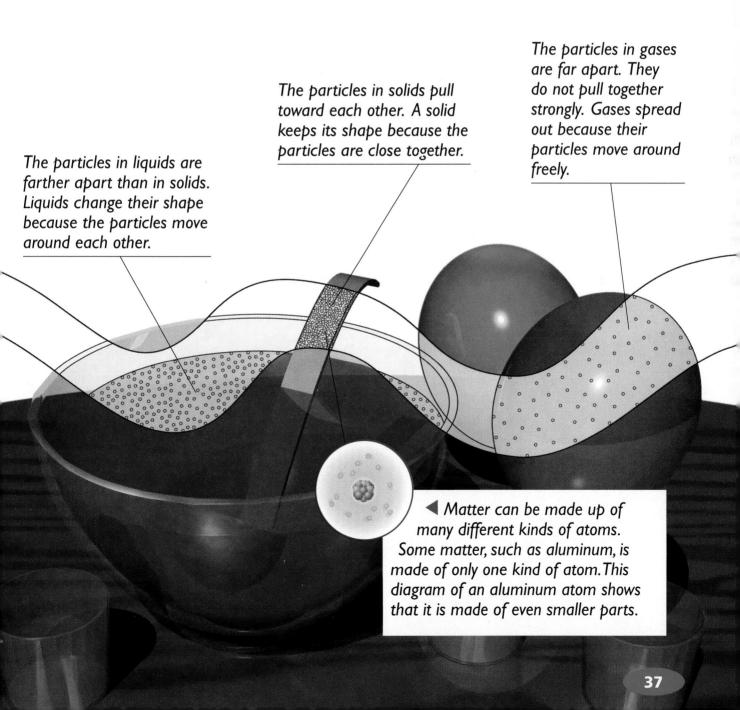

The particles in solids pull toward each other. A solid keeps its shape because the particles are close together.

The particles in gases are far apart. They do not pull together strongly. Gases spread out because their particles move around freely.

The particles in liquids are farther apart than in solids. Liquids change their shape because the particles move around each other.

◀ *Matter can be made up of many different kinds of atoms. Some matter, such as aluminum, is made of only one kind of atom. This diagram of an aluminum atom shows that it is made of even smaller parts.*

Waves of Energy

Waves carry energy from one place to another. Sound and light are forms of energy that move as waves. You can see some waves, such as waves in water. Other waves, such as sound waves, are invisible.

◄ *Sound waves move out from a gong after it has been hit. The sound waves travel from the vibrating gong through the air to your ear.*

When you drop a stone into water, waves of energy travel through the water. The energy waves move out from the center in the form of circles. ▼

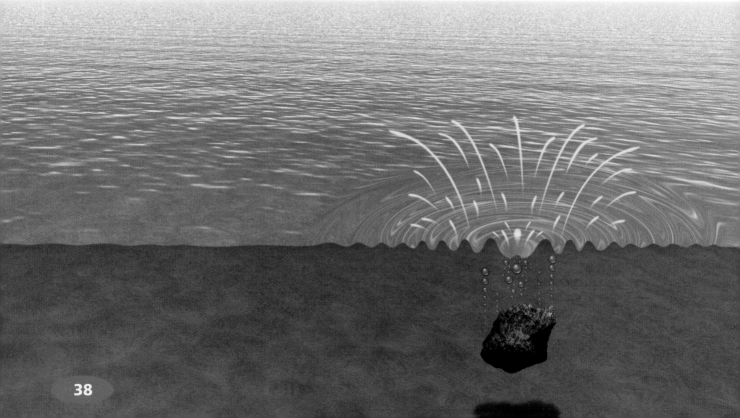

Colors of White Light

The light that we see is known as white light. White light really is made up of many different colors.

Light energy travels in waves. The colors that make up white light can be separated into a band of different colors. This band is called the visible spectrum. The seven colors of the visible spectrum are red, orange, yellow, green, blue, indigo, and violet.

▶ A prism, or piece of glass or plastic shaped like a triangle, can separate white light into the colors of the visible spectrum.

◀ You see a rainbow when raindrops in the air bend the light waves coming from the sun. The sunlight is separated into the different colored parts of the visible spectrum.

Systems

A system is a set of things that form a whole. Systems can be made of many different parts. All the parts depend on each other. The whole system works because all the parts work together.

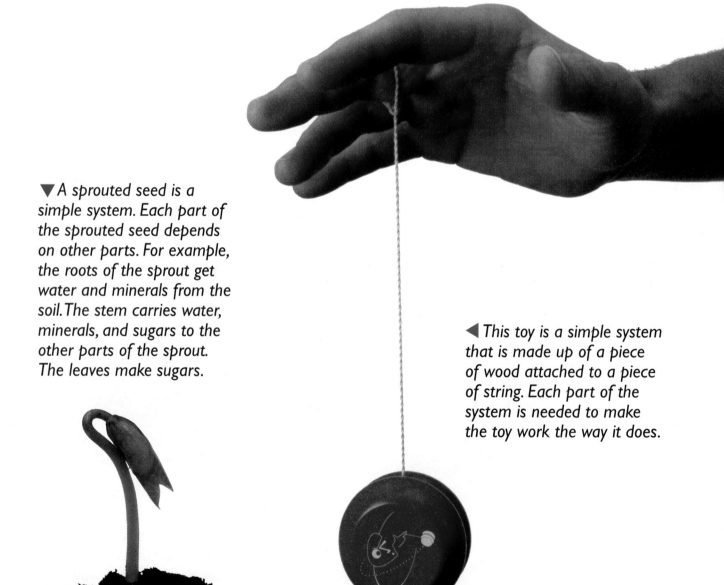

▼ *A sprouted seed is a simple system. Each part of the sprouted seed depends on other parts. For example, the roots of the sprout get water and minerals from the soil. The stem carries water, minerals, and sugars to the other parts of the sprout. The leaves make sugars.*

◄ *This toy is a simple system that is made up of a piece of wood attached to a piece of string. Each part of the system is needed to make the toy work the way it does.*

◀ This ecosystem is an example of a system that contains living things. The parts of the system that interact and depend on each other are the plants and the buffalo.

◀ The fish, plants, water, and oxygen in this aquarium all depend on each other to make the system work.

Layers of the Earth

Atmosphere

A blanket of air, called the atmosphere, surrounds the earth. The earth's atmosphere protects it from harmful sunlight and helps organisms on the earth survive.

Crust

The earth itself is made of layers. The outer layer, or crust, of the earth is made up of rocks and soil. The land you walk on and the land under the oceans are part of the crust.

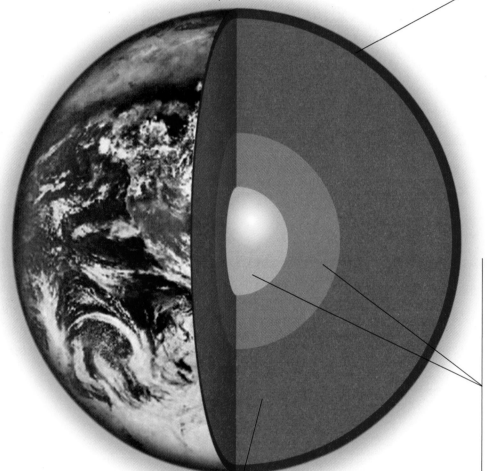

Core

The center of the earth—the core—is made mostly of iron. The outside part of the core has liquid iron. The inside part has solid iron. The core is the hottest part of the earth. The temperature of the core is almost as hot as the surface of the sun!

Mantle

The middle layer of the earth is called the mantle. The mantle is mostly made of rock. Some of the rock in the mantle is partly melted.

The Rock Cycle

In the rock cycle, rocks form and change into other types of rock. Rocks form in three main ways. Over millions of years, each type of rock can change into another type of rock.

Rocks that form from melted material deep inside the earth are igneous rocks. Granite is an igneous rock.

As a result of weathering, rocks break down. Sand and small bits of rock sink beneath the water. Layers of material press together underwater and form sedimentary rocks. Sandstone is a sedimentary rock.

Metamorphic rock forms as very high heat and great pressure within the earth change igneous and sedimentary rocks. Gneiss is a metamorphic rock.

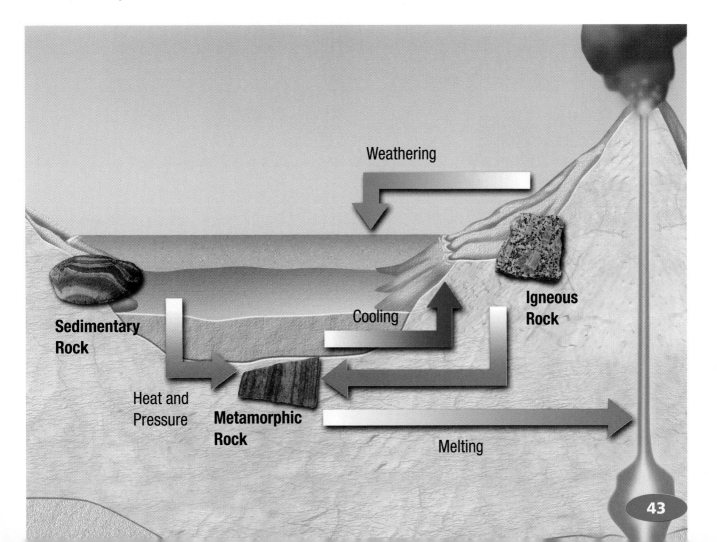

Weathering

Cooling

Igneous Rock

Sedimentary Rock

Heat and Pressure

Metamorphic Rock

Melting

Constellations

Long ago, people divided the stars in the sky into groups. They connected each group of stars with imaginary lines. The stars and lines looked like pictures in the sky. Each group of stars connected by imaginary lines is called a constellation.

The Big Dipper

Ursa Major or the Great Bear ▼

Canis Major ▼

Orion the Hunter ▲

Eclipses of the Sun and Moon

In an eclipse of the sun, or solar eclipse, the moon comes between the sun and Earth. The moon then makes a shadow form on Earth. Sometimes the moon blocks all of the sunlight from certain places on Earth. People in these places see a total solar eclipse. Daytime seems as dark as night. In other places, only some light is blocked. People there see a partial eclipse.

Solar Eclipse

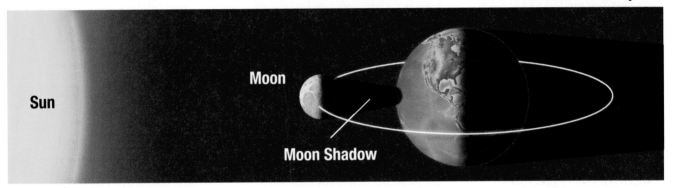

Sun

Moon

Moon Shadow

Sometimes Earth comes between the moon and the sun. When the moon moves through the shadow of Earth, an eclipse of the moon, or a lunar eclipse happens.

Lunar Eclipse

Sun

Moon

Earth Shadow

Natural Resources

Natural resources are useful materials that come from the earth. Natural resources can be renewable, nonrenewable, or inexhaustible.

▲ *Trees are a renewable resource. New trees can be planted to replace trees that have been cut down. It may take years, however, for the new trees to become fully grown. The soil that the trees grow in is also a renewable resource. Weathered rock and humus are always being added to soil.*

▲ *Some natural resources, such as gas and oil, are nonrenewable. They cannot be replaced. Once the supply of gas and oil from the earth is used up, these resources will be gone forever.*

▲ *Sunlight and water are examples of natural resources that can never be used up. They are known as inexhaustible natural resources.*

▶ *Wind is also an inexhaustible natural resource. Wind is being used here to make electric power.*

Tools

Tools can make objects appear larger. They can help you measure volume, temperature, length, distance, and mass. Tools can help you figure out amounts and analyze your data. Tools can also provide you with the latest scientific information.

You can figure amounts using a calculator.▶

▲ *Safety goggles protect your eyes.*

◀ *Microscopes have several lenses to make objects appear larger. Use a microscope to analyze materials that your teacher provides. Describe the details that you might not have been able to see with just your eyes.*

▲ *A hand lens makes objects appear larger so you can see more details.*

▶ You use a thermometer to measure temperature. Many thermometers have both Farenheit and Celsius scales. Usually scientists only use the Celsius scale when measuring temperature.

▲ Computers can quickly provide the latest scientific information.

Scientists use metric rulers and meter sticks to measure length and distance. Scientists use the metric units of meters, centimeters, and millimeters to measure length and distance. ▼

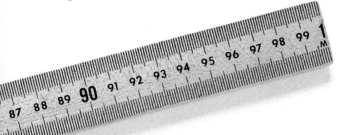

▼ Use a camera to collect and analyze information about a plant. Take a picture of a green plant that is near a sunny window. Do not move or turn the plant. Take another picture of it a week later. Compare the pictures to see if the plant has changed.

Clocks are used for measuring time. ▼

▲ *You can talk into a tape recorder to record information you want to remember. Use a tape recorder to collect and analyze information about the sounds of different kinds of birds. Then see if your classmates can identify the birds.*

▲ *You use a balance to measure mass.*

▲ *You can use a magnet to test whether an object is made of certain metals such as iron.*

▲*A compass is used to indicate direction. The directions on a compass include north, south, east, and west.*

Life Science

Physical Science

● **3000 B.C.**
The Egyptians develop geometry. They use it to re-measure their farmlands after floods of the Nile River.

Earth Science

● **8000 B.C.** Farming communities start as people use the plow for farming.

Human Body

4th century B.C.
Aristotle classifies
plants and animals.

3rd century B.C.
Aristarchus proposes that the
earth revolves around the sun.

4th century B.C.
Aristotle describes the
motions of falling
bodies. He believes that
heavier things fall faster
than lighter things.

260 B.C. Archimedes
discovers the principles of
buoyancy and the lever.

4th century B.C. Aristotle
describes the motions
of the planets.

200 B.C. Eratosthenes calculates
the size of the earth. His result is
very close to the earth's actual
size.

87 B.C.
Chinese report observing
an object in the sky that
later became known as
Halley's comet.

5th and 4th centuries B.C.
Hippocrates and other Greek
doctors record the symptoms of
many diseases. They also urge
people to eat a well-balanced diet.

**Life
Science**

**Physical
Science**

83 A.D.
Chinese travelers
use the compass
for navigation.

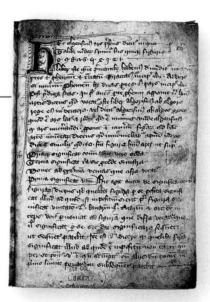

**About
750–1250**
Islamic scholars get
scientific books
from Europe. They
translate them into
Arabic and add
more information.

**Earth
Science**

140 Claudius Ptolemy
draws a complete picture of
an earth-centered universe.

132 The Chinese make the
first seismograph, a device
that measures the strength
of earthquakes.

**Human
Body**

2nd century Galen
writes about anatomy
and the causes of
diseases.

1100s
Animal guide books begin to appear. They describe what animals look like and give facts about them.

1250
Albert the Great describes plants and animals in his book *On Vegetables and On Animals*.

1555
Pierre Belon finds similarities between the skeletons of humans and birds.

9th century
The Chinese invent block printing. By the 11th century, they had movable type.

1019
Abu Arrayhan Muhammad ibn Ahmad al'Biruni observed both a solar and lunar eclipse within a few months of each other.

1543
Nikolaus Copernicus publishes his book *On The Revolutions of the Celestial Orbs*. It says that the sun remains still and the earth moves in a circle around it.

1265
Nasir al-Din al-Tusi gets his own observatory. His ideas about how the planets move will influence Nikolaus Copernicus.

About 1000
Ibn Sina writes an encyclopedia of medical knowledge. For many years, doctors will use this as their main source of medical knowledge. Arab scientist Ibn Al-Haytham gives the first detailed explanation of how we see and how light forms images in our eyes.

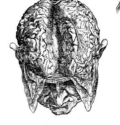

1543
Andreas Vesalius publishes *On the Makeup of the Human Body*. In this book he gives very detailed pictures of human anatomy.

53

1600	1620	1640	1660	1680

Life Science

1663 Robert Hooke first sees the cells of living organisms through a microscope. Antoni van Leeuwenhoek discovers bacteria with the microscope in 1674.

1679 Maria Sibylla Merian paints the first detailed pictures of a caterpillar turning into a butterfly. She also develops new techniques for printing pictures.

Physical Science

1600 William Gilbert describes the behavior of magnets. He also shows that the attraction of a compass needle toward North is due to the earth's magnetic pole.

1632 Galileo Galilei shows that all objects fall at the same speed. Galileo also shows that all matter has inertia.

1687 Isaac Newton introduces his three laws of motion.

Earth Science

1609–1619 Johannes Kepler introduces the three laws of planetary motion.

1610 Galileo uses a telescope to see the rings around the planet Saturn and the moons of Jupiter.

1669 Nicolaus Steno sets forth the basic principles of how to date rock layers.

1650 Maria Cunitz publishes a new set of tables to help astronomers find the positions of the planets and stars.

1693–1698 Maria Eimmart draws 250 pictures depicting the phases of the moon. She also paints flowers and insects.

1687 Isaac Newton introduces the concept of gravity.

Human Body

1628 William Harvey shows how the heart circulates blood through the blood vessels.

54

1735 Carolus Linnaeus devises the modern system of naming living things.

1759 Emile du Châtelet translates Isaac Newton's work into French. Her work still remains the only French translation.

1789 Antoine-Laurent Lavoisier claims that certain substances, such as oxygen, hydrogen, and nitrogen, cannot be broken down into anything simpler. He calls these substances "elements."

1704 Isaac Newton publishes his views on optics. He shows that white light contains many colors.

1729 Stephen Gray shows that electricity flows in a straight path from one place to another.

1781 Caroline and William Herschel (sister and brother) discover the planet Uranus.

1784 French chemist Antoine-Laurent Lavoisier does the first extensive study of respiration.

1798 Edward Jenner reports the first successful vaccination for smallpox.

1721 Onesimus introduces to America the African method for inoculation against smallpox.

1805　1810　1815　1820　1825　1830　1835

Life Science

1808 French naturalist Georges Cuvier describes some fossilized bones as belonging to a giant, extinct marine lizard.

1838–1839 Matthias Schleiden and Theodor Schwann describe the cell as the basic unit of a living organism.

Physical Science

1800 Alessandro Volta makes the first dry cell (battery).

1820 H.C. Oersted discovers that a wire with electric current running through it will deflect a compass needle. This showed that electricity and magnetism were related.

1808 John Dalton proposes that all matter is made of atoms.

Earth Science

1830 Charles Lyell writes *Principles of Geology*. This is the first modern geology textbook.

1803 Luke Howard assigns to clouds the basic names that we still use today—cumulus, stratus, and cirrus.

Human Body

1842 Richard Owen gives the name "dinosaurs" to the extinct giant lizards.

1859 Charles Darwin proposes the theory of evolution by natural selection.

1863 Gregor Mendel shows that certain traits in peas are passed to succeeding generations in a regular fashion. He outlines the methods of heredity.

1847 Hermann Helmholtz states the law of conservation of energy. This law holds that energy cannot be created or destroyed. Energy only can be changed from one form to another.

1842 Christian Doppler explains why a car, train, plane, or any quickly moving object sounds higher pitched as it approaches and lower pitched as it moves away.

1866 Ernst Haeckel proposes the term "ecology" for the study of the environment.

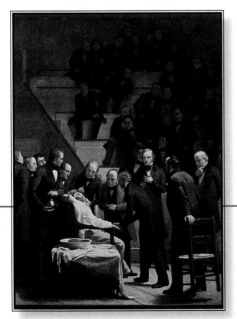

Early 1860s Louis Pasteur realizes that tiny organisms cause wine and milk to turn sour. He shows that heating the liquids kills these germs. This process is called pasteurization.

1840s Doctors use anesthetic drugs to put their patients to sleep.

1850s and 1860s Ignaz P. Semmelweis and Sir Joseph Lister pioneer the use of antiseptics in medicine.

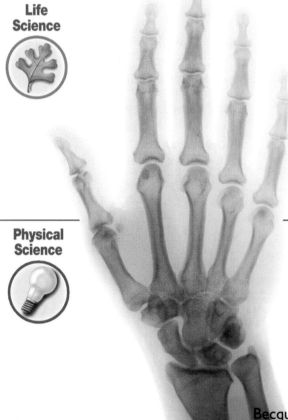

1875 **1885** **1895** **1905**

Life Science

1900–1910 George Washington Carver, the son of slave parents, develops many new uses for old crops. He finds a way to make soybeans into rubber, cotton into road-paving material, and peanuts into paper.

Physical Science

1897 J. J. Thomson discovers the electron.

1905 Albert Einstein introduces the theory of relativity.

1895 Wilhelm Roentgen discovers X rays.

1896 Henri Becquerel discovers radioactivity.

Earth Science

1907 Bertram Boltwood introduces the idea of "radioactive" dating. This allows geologists to accurately measure the age of a fossil.

1912 Alfred Wegener proposes the theory of continental drift. This theory says that all land on the earth was once a single mass. It eventually broke apart and the continents slowly drifted away from each other.

Human Body

1885 Louis Pasteur gives the first vaccination for rabies. Pasteur thought that tiny organisms caused most diseases.

58

1920s Ernest Everett Just performs important research into how cells metabolize food.

1947 Archaeologist Mary Leakey unearths the skull of a *Proconsul africanus,* an example of a fossilized ape.

1913 Danish physicist Niels Bohr presents the modern theory of the atom.

1911 Ernst Rutherford discovers that atoms have a nucleus, or center.

1911 Marie Curie wins the Nobel Prize for chemistry. This makes her the first person ever to win two Nobel Prizes, the highest award a scientist can receive.

1938 Otto Hahn and Fritz Straussman split the uranium atom. This marks the beginning of the nuclear age.

1942 Enrico Fermi and Leo Szilard produce the first nuclear chain reaction.

1945 The first atomic bomb is exploded in the desert at Alamogordo, New Mexico.

1938 Lise Meitner and Otto Frisch explain how an atom can split in two.

1946 Vincent Schaefer and Irving Langmuir use dry ice to produce the first artificial rain.

1933 Meteorologist Tor Bergeron explains how raindrops form in clouds.

1917 Florence Sabin becomes the first woman professor at an American medical college.

1928 Alexander Fleming notices that the molds in his petri dish produced a substance, later called an antibiotic, that killed bacteria. He calls this substance penicillin.

1935 Chemist Percy Julian develops physostigmine, a drug used to fight the eye disease glaucoma.

1922 Doctors inject the first diabetes patient with insulin.

1950	1955	1960	1965	1970

Life Science

1951 Barbara McClintock discovers that genes can move to different places on a chromosome.

1953 The collective work of James D. Watson, Francis Crick, Maurice Wilkins, and Rosalind Franklin leads to the discovery of the structure of the DNA molecule.

1972 Researchers find human DNA to be 99% similar to that of chimpanzees.

Physical Science

1969 UCLA is host to the first computer node of ARPANET, the forerunner of the internet.

1974 Opening of TRIUMF, the world's largest particle accelerator, at the University of British Columbia.

Earth Science

1957 The first human-made object goes into orbit when the Soviet Union launches *Sputnik I*.

1972 Cygnus X-1 is first identified as a blackhole.

1969 Neil Armstrong is the first person to walk on the moon.

1967 Geophysicists introduce the theory of plate tectonics.

1962 John Glenn is the first American to orbit the earth.

Human Body

1954–1962 In 1954, Jonas Salk introduced the first vaccine for polio. In 1962, most doctors and hospitals substituted Albert Sabin's orally administered vaccine.

1967 Dr. Christiaan Barnard performs the first successful human heart transplant operation.

1964 The surgeon general's report on the hazards of smoking is released.

NO SMOKING
American Cancer Society

1988
Congress approves funding for the Human Genome Project. This project will map and sequence the human genetic code.

1997
Scientists in Edinburgh, Scotland, successfully clone a sheep, Dolly.

1975 People are able to buy the first personal computer, called the Altair.

1996 Scientists make "element 112" in the laboratory. This is the heaviest element yet created.

1979 A near meltdown occurs at the Three Mile Island nuclear power plant in Pennsylvania. This alerts the nation to the dangers of nuclear power.

Early 1990s The first "extra-solar" planet is discovered.

1995 The National Severe Storms Laboratory develops NEXRAD, the national network of Doppler weather radar stations for early severe storm warnings.

1976 National Academy of Sciences reports on the dangers of chlorofluorocarbons (CFCs) for the earth's ozone layer.

1981 The first commercial Magnetic Resonance Imaging scanners are available. Doctors use MRI scanners to look at the non-bony parts of the body.

1982 Dr. Stanley Prusiner identifies a new kind of disease-causing agent—prions. Prions are responsible for many brain disorders.

1998 John Glenn, age 77, orbits the earth aboard the space shuttle *Discovery*. Glenn is the oldest person to fly in space.

Glossary

Full Pronunciation Key

The pronunciation of each word is shown just after the word, in this way: **ab·bre·vi·ate** (ə brē′vē āt).

The letters and signs used are pronounced as in the words below.

The mark ′ is placed after a syllable with primary or heavy accent, as in the example above.

The mark ′ after a syllable shows a secondary or lighter accent, as in **ab·bre·vi·a·tion** (ə brē′vē ā′shən).

a	hat, cap	g	go, bag	ō	open, go	ŦH	then, smooth	zh	measure, seizure
ā	age, face	h	he, how	ȯ	all, caught	u	cup, butter		
â	care, fair	i	it, pin	ô	order	ù	full, put	ə	represents:
ä	father, far	ī	ice, five	oi	oil, voice	ü	rule, move		a in about
b	bad, rob	j	jam, enjoy	ou	house, out	v	very, save		e in taken
ch	child, much	k	kind, seek	p	paper, cup	w	will, woman		i in pencil
d	did, red	l	land, coal	r	run, try				o in lemon
e	let, best	m	me, am	s	say, yes	y	young, yet		u in circus
ē	equal, be	n	no, in	sh	she, rush	z	zero, breeze		
ėr	term, learn	ng	long, bring	t	tell, it				
f	fat, if	o	hot, rock	th	thin, both				

A

adaptation (ad′ap tā′shən), a structure or behavior that helps an organism survive in its environment.

alcohol (al′kə hȯl), a drug found in beer, wine, and liquor that can be harmful.

amphibian (am fib′ē ən), an animal with a backbone that lives part of its life cycle in water and part on land.

astronaut (as′trə nȯt), a person who travels in space.

atmosphere (at′mə sfir), air that surrounds the earth.

atom (at′əm), a small particle that makes up matter.

axis (ak′sis), an imaginary straight line through the center of Earth around which Earth rotates.

B

bacteria (bak tir′ē ə), organisms made of one cell that can be seen through a microscope.

bar graph, a graph that uses bars to show data.

blizzard (bliz′ərd), a snowstorm with strong, cold winds and very low temperatures.

C

caption (kap′shən), written material that helps explain a picture or diagram.

carbon dioxide (kär′bən dī ok′sīd), a gas in the air that plants use to make food.

cartilage (kär′tl ij), a tough, rubbery tissue that makes up parts of the skeleton.

cause (kȯz), a person, thing, or event that makes something happen.

cell (sel), the basic unit of all living things, including the human body.

chemical (kem′ə kəl) **change**, a change that causes one kind of matter to become a different kind of matter.

circuit (sėr′kit), the path an electric current follows.

clay (klā) **soil**, soil with tiny grains that are packed closely together.

cloud, a mass of many water droplets or bits of ice that float in the air.

community (kə myü′nə tē), all the plants, animals, and other organisms that live and interact in the same place.

compare (kəm pâr′), to decide which of two numbers is greater.

conclusion (kən klü′zhən), a decision or opinion based on evidence and reasoning.

condense (kən dens′), to change from a gas to a liquid.

conductor (kən duk′tər), a material through which energy flows easily.

conifer (kon′ə fər), a tree or shrub that has cones.

conserve (kən sėrv′), to keep something from being used up.

consumer (kən sü′mər), an organism that eats food.

control (kən trōl′), the part of an experiment that does not have the variable being tested.

core (kôr), the center part of the earth.

crater (krā′tər), a large hole in the ground that is shaped like a bowl.

crust (krust), the solid outside part of the earth.

D

data (dā′tə), information.

decay (di kā′), to slowly break down or rot.

decomposer (dē′kəm pō′zər), a living thing that feeds on the wastes or dead bodies of other living things and breaks them down.

disease (də zēz′), an illness.

drought (drout), a long period of dry weather.

E

eardrum (ir′drum′), the thin, skinlike layer that covers the middle part of the ear and vibrates when sound reaches it.

earthquake (ėrth′kwāk′), a shaking or sliding of the surface of the earth.

echo (ek′ō), a sound that bounces back from an object.

effect (ə fekt′), whatever is produced by a cause; a result.

electric charges (i lek′trik chär′jəz), tiny amounts of electricity present in all matter.

electric circuit (i lek′trik sėr′kit), the path along which electric current moves.

electric current (i lek′trik kėr′ənt), the flow of electric charges.

electromagnet (i lek′trō mag′nit), a metal that becomes a magnet when electricity passes through wire wrapped around it.

embryo (em′brē ō), a developing animal before it is born or hatched.

endangered (en dān′jərd) **organism**, a kind of living thing of which very few exist and that someday might not be found on the earth.

energy (en′ər jē), the ability to do work.

energy of motion (mō′shən), energy that moving objects have.

environment (en vī′rən mənt), all the things that surround an organism.

erosion (i rō′zhən), the carrying away of weathered rocks or soils by water, wind, or other causes.

erupt (i rupt′), to burst out.

evaporates (i vap′ə rāts), changes from a liquid state to a gas state.

extinct (ek stingkt′) **organism**, a kind of living thing that is no longer found on the earth.

F

food chain, the way food passes from one organism to another.

force (fôrs), a push or a pull.

fossil (fos′əl), the hardened parts or marks left by an animal or plant that lived long ago.

friction (frik′shən), the force caused by two objects rubbing together that slows down or stops moving objects.

fuel (fyü′əl), a material that is burned to produce useful heat.

fulcrum (ful′krəm), the point on which a lever is supported and moves.

fungus (fung′gəs), an organism, such as a mold or mushroom, that gets food from dead material or by growing on food or a living thing.

G

gas, a state in which matter has no definite shape or volume.

gear (gir), a wheel with jagged edges like teeth.

germ (jėrm), a thing too tiny to be seen without a microscope; some germs may cause disease.

germinate (jėr′mə nāt), to begin to grow and develop.

gills (gilz), the parts of fish and tadpoles that are used to take in oxygen from water.

glacier (glā′shər), a huge amount of moving ice.

graphic sources (graf′ik sôrs′əz), pictures or diagrams that give information.

gravity (grav′ə tē), the force that pulls objects toward the center of the earth.

H

habitat (hab′ə tat), the place where an organism lives.

humus (hyü′məs), decayed organisms in soil.

hurricane (hėr′ə kän), a huge storm that forms over warm ocean water, with strong winds and heavy rains.

I

illegal (i lē′gəl) **drug**, a drug that is against the law to buy, sell, or use.

inclined plane (in klīnd′ plān), a simple machine that is a flat surface with one end higher than the other.

instinct (in′stingkt), an action that an animal can do without learning.

insulator (in′sə lā′tər), a material through which energy cannot flow easily.

involuntary (in vol′ən ter′ē) **muscle**, the kind of muscle that works without a person's control.

J

joint, the place where two bones come together.

L

landfill (land′fil′), a place where garbage is buried in soil.

landform (land′fôrm′), a shape on the earth's surface.

larva (lär′və), a young animal that has a different shape than the adult.

lava (lä′və), hot, melted rock that comes out of a volcano.

lens (lenz), a piece of material that bends light rays that pass through it.

lever (lev′ər), a simple machine made of a bar or board that is supported underneath at the fulcrum.

life cycle (sī′kəl), the stages in the life of a living thing.

ligament (lig′ə mənt), a strong, flexible tissue that holds bones together at a joint.

liquid (lik′wid), a state in which matter has a definite volume but no shape of its own.

liter (lē′tər), a metric unit of volume or capacity equal to 1,000 mL.

loam (lōm), good planting soil that is a mixture of clay, silt, sand, and humus.

M

magma (mag′mə), hot, melted rock and gases deep inside the earth.

magnet (mag′nit), anything that pulls certain metals, such as iron, to it.

magnetism (mag′nə tiz′əm), the force that causes magnets to pull on objects that are made of certain metals, such as iron.

mammal (mam′əl), an animal with a backbone and hair or fur; mothers produce milk for their babies.

mass, the measure of how much matter an object contains.

matter, anything that takes up space and has weight.

milliliter (mil′ə lē′tər), a metric unit of volume or capacity smaller than a liter.

mineral (min′ər əl), a nonliving material that can be found in soil.

mixture (miks′chər), two or more kinds of matter that are placed together but can be easily separated.

muscle (mus′əl), a body tissue that can tighten or loosen to move body parts.

N

natural resource (nach′ər′əl rē′sôrs), a material that comes from the earth and can be used by living things.

nerve (nėrv), a part of the body that carries messages to the brain.

nicotine (nik′ə tēn′), a drug in tobacco that can harm the body.

nutrient (nü′trē ənt), a mineral that plants and animals need to live and grow; a substance in food that living things need for health and growth.

nymph (nimf), a stage in an insect life cycle between egg and adult that looks like an adult but has no wings.

O

orbit (ôr′bit), the path an object follows as it moves around another object.

ore (or), rock that has a large amount of useful minerals.

organ (ôr′gən), a body part that does a special job within a body system.

organism (ôr′gə niz′əm), a living thing.

over-the-counter medicine (med′ə sən), a medicine that can be bought without a doctor's order.

oxygen (ok′sə jən), a gas in air that living things need to stay alive.

P

petal (pet′l), an outside part of a flower that is often colored.

phase (fāz), the shape of the lighted part of the moon.

physical (fiz′ə kəl) **change**, a change in the way matter looks, but the kind of matter remains the same.

pictograph (pik′tə graf), a graph that uses pictures or symbols to show data.

pitch (pich), how high or low a sound is.

plain (plān), a large, flat area of land.

planet (plan′it), a large body of matter that moves around a star such as the sun.

plateau (pla tō′), a large flat area of land that is high.

pole (pōl), a place on a magnet where magnetism is strongest.

pollen (pol′ən), a fine, yellowish powder in a flower.

pollinate (pol′ə nāt), to carry pollen to the stemlike part of the flower.

pollution (pə lü′shən), anything harmful added to the air, water, or land.

population (pop′yə lā′shən), organisms of the same kind that live in the same place at the same time.

precipitation (pri sip′ə tā′shən), a form of water that falls to the ground from clouds.

predator (pred′ə tər), an organism that captures and eats other organisms.

prediction (pri dik′shən), an idea about what will happen based on evidence.

prescription medicine (pri skrip′shən med′ə sən), a medicine that can be bought only with a doctor's order.

prey (prā), an organism that is captured and eaten by another organism.

producer (prə dü′sər), an organism that makes its own food.

property (prop′ər tē), something about an object—such as size, shape, color, or smell—that you can observe with one or more of your senses.

pulley (púl′ē), a simple machine made of a wheel and a rope.

pupa (pyü′pə), the stage in the insect life cycle between larva and adult.

R

ray, a thin line of light.

recycle (rē sī′kəl), to change something so it can be used again.

reflect (ri flekt′), to bounce back.

revolution (rev′ə lü′shən), movement of an object in an orbit around another object.

rotate (rō′tāt), to spin on an axis.

S

sandy (san′dē) **soil,** loose soil with large grains.

satellite (sat′l īt), an object that revolves around another object.

scale, the numbers that show the units used on a bar graph.

screw (skrü), a simple machine used to hold objects together.

seed coat (sēd kōt), the outside covering of a seed.

seed leaf (sēd lēf), the part inside each seed that contains stored food.

seedling (sēd′ling), a young plant that grows from a seed.

sequence (sē′kwens), one thing happening after another.

simple machine (sim′pəl mə shēn′), one of six kinds of tools with few or no moving parts that make work easier.

solar system (sō′lər sis′təm), the sun, the planets and their moons, and other objects that move around the sun.

solid (sol′id), a state in which matter has a definite shape and volume.

star (stär), a very large mass of hot, glowing gases,

states of matter, the three forms of matter—solid, liquid, and gas.

stored (stôrd) **energy,** energy that can change later into a form that can do work.

system (sis′təm), a group of body parts that work together to perform a job.

T

tadpole (tad′pōl), a very young frog or toad.

telescope (tel′ə skōp), an instrument for making distant objects appear nearer and larger.

temperature (tem′per ə chər), a measure of how hot a place or object is.

tendon (ten′dən), a strong cord of tissue that attaches a muscle to a bone.

tide (tīd), the rise and fall of the ocean, mainly due to the moon's gravity.

tissue (tish′ü), a group of cells that look alike and work together to do a certain job.

tornado (tôr nā′dō), a funnel cloud that has very strong winds and moves along a narrow path.

V

vaccine (vak sēn′), a medicine that can prevent the disease caused by one kind of germ.

vibrate (vī′brāt), move quickly back and forth.

vocal cords (vō′kəl kôrdz), two small folds of elastic tissue at the top of the windpipe.

volcano (vol kā′nō), a type of mountain that has an opening at the top through which lava, ash, or other types of volcanic rock flows.

volume (vol′yəm), the amount of space an object takes up; the loudness or softness of a sound.

voluntary muscle (vol′ən ter′ē mus′əl), the kind of muscle that a person can control.

W

water cycle (sī′kəl), movement of water from the earth to the air and back to the earth.

water vapor (vā′pər), water that is in the form of a gas.

weathering (weTH′ər ing), the breaking apart and changing of rocks.

wedge (wej), a simple machine used to cut or split an object.

wheel and axle (wēl and ak′səl), a simple machine that has a center rod attached to a wheel.

work (wėrk), something done whenever a force moves an object through a distance.

Index